Fragments
of
Intent

(From the First Three Fountains)
(Healing Hearts Version)

Robert J. Koyich

Copyright © 2018 Robert James Koyich

All rights reserved.

ISBN-13: 978-1-989180-01-3

DEDICATION

From a seed to a star, we learn who we are.

CONTENTS

Finding Natalie

From Natalie's Perspective	1
From Some Other's Perspective	11
What Does it Matter?	21
From the Soul to the Spirit	31
What Were You Doing Robert?	41
Rite from the Sprite	47
A Fragment of Intent	55

Searching for Tomorrow

What Would You Like to Know?	59
Build With Someone	65
Dare to Dream	73
Take a Breath	81
Draw the Mana	89
Some Questions to Ask	99
What I'm Doing, and Why	105

ROBERT KOYICH

From the Valley to the Fountain

To the Original Lovestone   113

I'm an Addict   121

Continue to Learn   131

Another Fragment of Intent   139

Acknowledgments   147

Books, Contact Info, and Links   149

FROM NATALIE'S PERSPECTIVE

Kevin Morris is a significant shoulsman in this story. A shoulsman is an honourable male, and Kevin gave Rob an excuse to stay up late and help us create. Although so much is on the plate, the facts of tact's selection also assure we don't take a ruse cruise. While fused to the thoughts held in Stream by the dream, we help weld the team to this cell, or so it is to seem.

A whisper louder than a sacred, solemn scream finds the kinds of things that bring the Kings under wings. The pings of seeds heed the needs of a vassal as we castle a few ideas. What stems from Rob's friend are the purposes of adoption and love and life.

Although the flows Rob's recorded have been in some ears too often, it's true that the heart does soften. Like a nail in the coffin, do not be scoffing at the magnitude of this dude's gumption. Clarify each assumption made and find the spade dig deep in the page made to scriggle what we think into ink. Discover how others like Ross had forced the link.

While coffee a preferred drink, Rob drank an Earl Grey tea before writing to me. It's true that Triangle, my website, said that my favourite movie was 'Big Blue' way back before the first digit of our year was 2. Though a trip to Japan was in the plan, some others influence the decisions made. This book, work, and stage are prayed to thank you all for allowing us to have seeded that kept in the hands of fate. I must wait.

The music said, "I was talking to my darkest shadows" when he wrote this for me. Some say that each line holds the key to open the door. It's how the love was known years before they recorded *The Score* in the war, yet these things may not be true. I still don't know the friend who drew a picture posted in Rob's kitchen. His cats were held well by ones who loved them; even when they meowed so much. Now calls from the past cast outwit and outlast one who's also allowed to drive, yet has no car. "Yarr!"

I don't yet know how or when we'll meet the people mentioned in this book. He seems to think there are so many and so few, yet only ever one of you.

This chapter's pages formed with me in mind, yet some of the names mentioned have been treated unkindly. Possibly, Rob had inclined this to be designed to wind into how I don't yet know any of the people held on his side of the table. From *Fable* and *Torn*, the song's intents of Hong Kong are known to disguise some who help share and show the original reprise. It's a flow from which we continue to grow.

When Rob wrote this for me, some of the people held the key to the glee and joy of his baby boy. I've been to some similar places as Rob has and note that, when written, we hadn't yet both seen each other's faces. Mine showed with the bright blue eyes. A note from Lisa Lobe glows in the disguise of how the globe is still the same size. People may connect so much more easily technologically than we could in 1998.

"Each artist needs a place to create."

Some find places like Darling Harbor in Sydney, Australia like

Rob had for New Year's 2010-2011. That night was magnificent from his perception, and he believed it was destiny for us to have met that night. "Maybe I'm not ready?" and he knows that we were not. Deeper in the plan that could ever be the plot.

Rob seems to think himself a misguided youth that has dreams that people cannot comprehend. Keep in mind the depth of which we tend comes to send that he's to lend and be a friend. What's written for me to read must be fact according to the author's design, yet misinterpretation may share and nudge some signs along the way; the paint that I, Aquarius, has yet to let us pray.

He doesn't know my opinions, likes, or thoughts. As far as Rob's aware, there's no fact I'll even read this. The truth of *Here to There* shares a sizeable Gund bear named Nancy. She wears a wizard hat on the top of Rob's bookshelf where had lived two beautiful and amazing cats. One was called Winks, and the other Boots. While the cursor scoots across the pages brought up to stages of introduction, some functions cipher well on the other side of this, Belle.

As well as True, other names should be given to complete the code's base. The first cat was known years before the kitten's purr as Minou. Rob has photos of Minou, his Mom, and himself the morning his Mom found the bong. The three of them lived together in junior high and high school without his Dad. Minou was a calico, though the sad thing is some animals and people have been abused.

Into my awareness seeps a tainted soul; a torrent of lost control and bowl after bowl after bowl. Rob's afraid of letting me know his fears and pushing me away, yet on the other side of the equation it's a good thing it's up to me to choose. I shall read and hear and not yet respond to the dream; a dream that has sometimes been an utterly one-sided obsession and irrational belief.

Why would I ever want to be with someone who's done so much wrong and has loved so many terrible things? I guess there's solace in knowing that I can read all about it and then set the book on fire. *"Concern about how we burn and doubt that we learn."* Way too cryptic, Robert.

Sometimes it seems that the dreams *are* to tear apart the streams; a continual obsessive focal point I wish not to be. With certainty, there *is* only one of you or me, and there are billions of other humans on this planet too.

Why would I search for someone who I've never even known; one who's said and done so many things of which I don't approve? How can they believe it *is* love when they haven't even met me? I suppose it goes back to how one does share a bit of themselves when they make an album; at least sometimes.

Who does he think I am anyway? Rob's never had the chance to ask me a question, he's never heard me share a story with a friend, and he certainly doesn't yet know anyone else that I know. When Rob wrote this, he still had no idea even how to greet me, how to earn his own life, or even how to love; or so I had thought.

I guess if we're reading this, though, Rob has made a bit of a journey. Still, why am *I* reading this?! Maybe I should just put this book down and read later… or perhaps I should turn to the last page and see the closing remarks… or, perhaps I was never given this book. Maybe I never took the time to read the book or it was never completed and is just another grain of sand along the shoreline. Perchance, though, Rob does love me.

"With the waves crashing in, I shed my fear and sin."

Even if a star keeps the planets near it warm, it too may be seen millions of light years away, maybe even by other lifeforms on the cold side of their world. A mention of the Mindstone, miss Jackson, yet what is for real? I combine a trine with Scentsy line; trademarks made for us within the sign!

This kid writes other book ideas. One is a bunch of his information, thoughts, story and opinions called *Beautiful, Do You Mind?* and another called *Built from Within. Finding Natalie* was the first one he wrote.

"It takes two to write, and one to read."

A terrible beginning, yet if it starts beautiful and at its best, then may it only deteriorate? Then too, what if it starts awful and we find that that start fertilizes the sapling to grow and thrive? Will I ever even meet this person? Are they still so delusional to hear my ego flare and whisper? I wonder how they thought they could ever be with me! Maybe others think I am all high and mighty thinking I'm above a pauper like Rob. Then again, perhaps they're projecting, and I *am* kindly intrigued by this.

The key to love is reciprocation and reciprocity. With that in mind, I hope we continue. Some might say we should know the depth of how low they had gone, and into what depths of near insanity they went with me in mind and soul. I don't want to give a pity party, so what shall 'come and go away' as Oasis had known? Rob and I both know that we have no idea what will be, while it's also true there are fears he may never know, it's like me to stand side by side looking away to the skies.

We stand upon different levels and points of the ground as we travel through the maze. The nights and days are places of time and space tracing how we now have and haven't ever yet been together. He can imagine me calling, "get out of your comfort zone and meet someone else, Rob! You cannot be with me!", yet as Blind Melon guided, it's like *A Seed to a Tree*.

Even knowing I may never meet him, he continues through just to let us know the fanciful whims of a stellar child; one who smiled the tears and drank the years into his soul. There is no way he will ever let go of me, yet I don't know if that's okay. It's true that a heart trapped in love for another cannot grasp things entirely, at least according to what some believe. If I could only tell him that there is no chance, maybe he would save himself the drama and the journey of trying to meet.

The piano is a beautiful instrument that can drop the most amazing sounds to nest a voice. Sarah McLachlan, Chantal Kreviazuk, and Vanessa Carlton are three that show such delicate and powerful brilliance. They are people who use the keys to ease the soul with their creative control. Some of us understand the depth of spirit that maintains we each shall hear it.

FRAGMENTS OF INTENT

The stars and stories of our planet come from centuries and millennia before we had even existed to help form our lives. A multitude of soldiers sacrificed their lives for the cost of the freedom that Rob has confused with the claim that people should be allowed to live and love and thrive. It's true that people should be allowed to flourish, just not at the cost of another.

From some time ago, a flow for a show helps tow along the raft of this craft. Many have allowed the plowed field to hold good seed, yet the yields must heed well of our intuition. Missions and omissions have bound sound about the grout. There is truth in our youth that we all shall remember to sprout.

UMI Says. Home is where we may nest, and while blessed, there too are the rest that we live within. Some have friends closer than kin, and some live behind the dumpster bin. The fact some have lacked their basic needs find seeds sown held row on row, yet not like Flander's Fields. There's the truth from our youth about how the booth holds some searching for gold, while others only want the truth to be told.

Grow up old and wise and share a creative reprise with the rise and fall of breath. Katie and Beth. Joel and Seth. Again, people that you may not know. How can we use the incessant flow to allow us to be there and know we grow? Somehow I refuse to read this and find Bliss carry the line into the spines that mingle on a single myth.

What has been brought up to sup with tracks that share Chilliwack's perception? Some things Rob's not allowed to mention, yet intention of convention need not an intervention as we hold him in suspension. The particles of clay remind us to say this does matter — the whim results in catapults throwing us back over the wall. Calls made shift the mix of hearts in spade to travel through the next spring, winter, summer, and fall.

Although the air is cold, the bold stare of no one there is what allows the class to pass. We're into the view of how You, maybe, made this with us in mind. Even though lined to mix the cliques into the drums, the beat plumbs Rob's being into a sweet treat with the myth of needing a Maze of Ith.

It's true some things we hold onto are not right for us. Sometimes we know what's not good for us and still choose to do those things. What I may say now of "wants to go out with you cow" is somehow I always keep the star's heart continually telling the seed not to start. The charts hold an interlude of a rude, crude brood saying the turtles eat their food.

Now, what about the songs sung and the artists Rob's written to and about? I cannot say for I don't know. It's the truth there is a vast network of us on this planet, and it's true that some of you *have* met. Then too, Earth shows through the things we do. What has Rob done for the music industry or this planet? Rob's just a person who wants a life earned, and has had so many cigarettes burned.

Rob will never win in life if he keeps it all within. My experience in a continual turn of sin cannot link to the thought that brings the wings up to let the angels cry. Maybe we do guard ourselves against Heaven and Hell. Tears

FRAGMENTS OF INTENT

sobbed have bobbed back to the tracks we don't understand after years and fears of the CD. Please remember, you may never be me.

Maybe I should listen to and try to meet Rob. Since this chapter is from my perspective, the belief of the situation should not be tainted with the advice or opinion of another. It's true that Rob's been through a lot and was ready to go into a relationship, though I too don't know what Rob was thinking about the entire situation.

Perchance I should check in and get other people's side of the story. Then again, what do we know about this whole story and how it's progressed? I definitely should check in with as many sources as possible before contacting Rob directly. If I promise to meet Rob, and then don't, it could be crushing for him. Then again an *Instant Crush* is a part of where this stemmed.

Brandon too might have some information on Rob, yet this may be completely irrelevant. The two were chatting on Facebook when Rob's two cats were both loved and neglected. Their owner was out of the house so much, and though the cat's apartment held only one human at the time, there's are some good friends that visit. It's a place where Rob thrives in the night sometimes and often has riddled us with cigarettes and coffee.

A fact is a place of mental haven.

This saga holds much of our story, yet some of the people who've been in Rob's home are no longer welcome. There also are some Rob would love to visit again that haven't made the time to do so. Out the window is a church; a place sometimes visited, yet not so much recently. The groups that form there have allowed the crowds to keep at bay and some even give the grace to let others hope and play. Rob prays for the day his grandchildren will say and sing things of love and joy that none may ever take away.

Granny Bea has been gone for many years, and though the sunset clears the horizon, some things are reprising the situation of this subtle notation. Our rebuttal of the consecration aids the elevation — the shifts and rifts of time and place trace the aura to pace past space's fold. A divinity clings to the pings of those both decisive and bold.

Like the wings that allow us to fly to the coronas of our eye, the seasons and sky disguise the rise and fall with breath. The death of Grandma Jane holds the sanity to remain like tears in the rain. Return to the sound of that found and let sanity resound in the soul with our creative control.

FROM SOME OTHER'S PERSPECTIVES

Yes, it's too late to decide what we shall do when we've already done it. While white mana is symbolized by a sun, blue by a water drop, red by fire, black by a skull, and green mana by a tree, Rob told two of us next to him he wrote this for you, Natalie.

Rob's only told me a bit, though I also don't know what he truly wants to do. I also can't tell you what the truth is about him and other people in this town. He's spent a vast amount of money on Magic and also is getting a bit desperate about not having any credit. Rob was only working two nights a week and should have been studying for his school final on Tuesday. Instead, he was up from the day before at eight in the morning writing this for us.

Rob's tried to teach me his language, and I'll hopefully tell him more about what to write. I didn't yet know how this chapter had formed; I don't even know who'll read it, or if anyone else ever shall. Maybe it'll just be another whim tossed aside as we help you understand how to decide.

Lots of people may hang out, joke, and share stories, though there still is a lot hidden of each. There's a theory Rob has about the different forms of self, though, he could let you know later when he finds out. Speaking of finding out, I'll give you all the dirt on Rob if you ask, even if I don't know what the consequences will be. Correct, though, that some of the flow helps us tow along the songs and the wrongs made.

"Help us dig into the Earth with a heart of worth."

About six or seven days passed between the last paragraph and this one. Rob uses music a lot, and although I wasn't there to hear, he put an album into play just before typing the first word of the next sentence. Holy crap that kid smokes though! The night Rob started this chapter he burned near a pack and a half inside his apartment. He almost smoked Tanner and me out!

It was Tanner who coined a few terms we've heard and used at the local gaming shop where some play Magic. Linked through the black mana, the pull of cigarettes and breath has led to you, Beth. I didn't know that your character's name was that, though I too don't know about Katie, and that Rob was talking with her earlier in the day.

A few of us have worked at a local call centre, and although people quit and leave or gripe about it, it lets them have some money. I've had some patterns that make finding a job complicated, and that's what Rob should be doing. Instead, he's writing on the computer at near 4 AM in the morning! WTF?!

The album that was playing was 'Mos Def, and Talib Kweli are Black Star' when the first tar bar of this session extinguished. I don't know what they wished for, though the door closed on sin as this was in the bin. Seriously, why would Rob write a book just for one gal?! He's not going to make money off a book, though some others want to do that too.

"Through the cue to speak, the tracks we hear peak into the transparent window. No one knows why I shut the eye and listen to the sky."

FRAGMENTS OF INTENT

Some call me names, though I've not heard any insults about me as far as Rob's told. Rob said he thinks it's funny when Tanner and I argue, and I also should introduce him to my girlfriend. Rob's complained about me texting three ks instead of just okay and some other things in response to his messages. I think Rob's a bit too edgy and he did get bitter earlier. He got pissed off about people asking him for Magic cards. Though even I note he's made some good deals, this book is for you, Natalie, so I'll try to not go off about stuff that's not relevant.

Things that I should warn you about Rob? He gets a bit distant and sometimes doesn't say much. At other times he talks too much and rhymes a lot. He's complained a bit about me also about how I move when standing up close to people, and though he's given me car rides home, I bring my longboard just in case he can't drive.

Rob also repeats some of his jokes too much. He told me the joke about "Why do Elephants have four feet" joke again for, like, the fourth time yesterday night. Rob dropped me off at home and then went home and said he needs to find a job; something he said he'll do on Monday.

We must look at the situation to find what is real and or fake. Do you want to make a trip to see Rob? He didn't talk about you last night, though mentions you a bit recently. I don't have a clue about much of the story, as, when written, Rob hadn't told me the scope of the whole situation.

We've not talked too much about the card shop we were to open, though I thought of opening it in the next two years. We don't know who'll be owners, though we might not now.

Tanner and I were meant to move in as roommates, though now Tanner's talking about running up north which means he might be sitching out. I wonder if I should let someone else take the pen, though get a hold of me later on as I'll know much more later on in the course of this. The question then, is who you should hear from next?

Okay, Brandon suggested me to write to you, Miss Jane. I have work on Tuesday and Rob will probably get me a lift to work in the morning. I pulled a herniated disc about two weeks ago, and Bill said that that type of injury doesn't go away. I've had lots of physical ailments for the past few years, though need to work to pay the bills. I went through a lot of hard times through the recent years, and although I have a good job now, I've still got some issues.

I used to live in the suite next to Rob. We both had a pair of cats when we lived there; mine named Gabby and Peter, while Rob's were Winks and Boots. Kitties are great, though both of us lost both our cats in the past few years. Peter and Boots went a few years before Winks and Gabby who both died in the year before Rob started this book. Gabby was a Japanese Bobtail who lived for more than 19 years. She was declawed before I got her, though she'd still scratch on things even though she had no claws.

Rob and I both like our cats, though I spent more time with mine. Rob was often out of the house back then too when he worked for a warehouse. Though we weren't hanging out much when he worked there, we played a bit of Magic with two other friends. I met Tim and Ross through Rob, and we used to play Magic at Rob's place. It's kind of strange that we didn't hang out so much when living on the opposite side of the wall. Rob and I both smoke, and our first few meetings were outside across the patios of our apartments.

I had lost a great friend near when Rob and I first started to talk. I did and didn't know that Rob was a bit cautious about me; I used to be much darker and told Rob some stuff about things I'd done when I was younger that scared him a bit. I recall hearing a lot mentally from Rob through the walls. Rob blamed it on another, though I'm not so sure he was telling the truth. What I know about Rob now is that he helped me out with rides to work at 5 AM as we had a deal; if he gave me a ride to work, I'd buy him a pack of smokes.

Rob told me a while ago that he's getting a bit desperate with his money situation. He said he'd been running on a line of credit since he was working at Wendy's after the warehouse job in 2009. I'm not a person to push my opinion and like to keep some things to myself, so I'll not reveal too much, though I do know a lot.

Rob talks a lot sometimes and at other times doesn't say much at all. I also know that I probably remember more of what he's told to me than he believes. I have gone through some tough times, though haven't been as lucky as Rob with the government. Even though I had no job, and couldn't get one, I couldn't get welfare and have gone without for too long. Jenn Joyce hired me on at Starbucks, yet with my back and heart issues, it was *not* easy.

It wasn't easy when Gabby or Peter went, and I'm like an elephant; I don't forget things. I'll sign out for now, though note I know a great deal about Rob. If you have any questions, please ask!

My son has been incredibly irresponsible with life. I didn't know to what extent, though the night he shifted from the previous paragraph to my perspective he sent me a message about his money situation. At the time I knew he was terrible with money, though still didn't know to what extent. Although he'd paid $18,000 down on the mortgage of the apartment he bought in 2007, Rob also had accumulated a debt of as much money as spent on cigarettes through the course of his 18 years of smoking.

Although his mother and I don't like that he smokes, we also don't know how deep the addiction had taken him. At the cost of $10 per pack at one or more packages per day, 18 years is $60,000 plus. Okay, so maybe he's not that far in debt with his credit at this point, though if he didn't smoke and put the money towards his apartment, he'd have $60,000 set towards his place. Again when he wrote this, I didn't know the depth of the ocean of debt he's alluded to before. I don't know if I'm more mad, sad, or disappointed, though am surprised as his irresponsibility.

Rob went through many years of drug use. I don't know if anyone told you about that yet, though I recall sitting with him in a waiting room at the hospital in 1998 waiting for them to admit him to the hospital. Even worse, he went back into drug life after that first trip to the ward! He used to call and ask for money often although I could make a fair guess that he was spending money on drugs. I loathe the thought of how much he has merely burned up with nothing to show other than a pile of debt and a smoke ridden apartment.

I used to tell Rob not to say to people about the wrong things in his life, though, yes it's vital you know. Rob used to lie and has wasted much of himself to drugs and other foul creatures for his body; even still if just with coffee and cigarettes. He's fortunate to be alive, and I will not write of a light side about that. Rob has come close to death a few times and some things I cannot divulge. I know that Rob is still very much like an irresponsible child, though I think you should hear from his Mom.

I love him.

His Dad is right, though. He has been very irresponsible and still hides things from his father and me. I have done so much to help Rob, and he's still not enabled himself well enough on his journey of life. He used to lie to me a lot also. I would do things to support Rob and still do, though I've wanted Rob to earn his way through life.

I do not condone some of the things that he does, like how he smokes, though almost more importantly he hasn't always worked to earn his money. For the past few years, Rob has relied on governmental funds to support himself instead of finding a full-time job and working at it. He's taken some courses at university, though I think he should have a full-time job and earn his money. I certainly didn't know when Rob wrote this about his debt.

Rob's Dad and I tried to raise Rob with a strong work ethic. My first job was at Safeway when I was a teen, and I earned my way to retirement. Rob's Dad and I divorced when Rob was in grade eight, and I raised him from that point until he went away to Simon Fraser University after high school.

Rob and I always had food, and I worked my ass off to support him and myself. Rob went away to SFU and didn't do very well, and although dabbling in them when he was in high school, Rob consumed lots of drugs when he went to university. I knew Rob had smoked some marijuana when he was living with me in Edmonton (I remember finding a bong under the garden hose when leaving the house one morning), and it was also during high school that he started smoking cigarettes regularly.

Rob had a car when he was younger. He received help to buy the car when he was in high school, and I stressed the importance that he should not drive drunk or worse. The rule was that if Rob had had anything to drink (or smoked) that I would pick up him *and* those he was driving, drop each of them off, and then go pick up the car the next day with no questions asked. Still, Rob hid many of his actions from me.

A note to you, even if I don't know you; Rob is still developing and learning. I hope he finds his path; it just saddens me that he hasn't discovered it yet.

I was the next person that Rob mentioned in his song *Digital Slipstate* by my actual name (not an abbreviation) other than himself.

My business partner and I hired Rob in June 2005 part-time for our (then) franchise branch of Nedco and Lite-Scape. He worked for us until April 2009 when we laid him and our outside sales person off at the same time. We hadn't spoken to him in the past years, though we know a lot about him from when he worked with us.

FRAGMENTS OF INTENT

When Rob first started with us, we were moving between our location on Railway into the first Harvard Place location. Ashton also worked for us at that time. We kept Rob around for a few years and even tried to include him in our lives outside of work too.

On one of his first few days, I invited Rob over to dinner with my family, although he declined. I didn't know that Rob refused because he was afraid, though that kind of set the tone of Rob being separate from us. My birthday was in the first week that Rob had started working for us and recall the puppet show that Ashton put on in the upper window. We liked Ashton a lot, and he worked well for us even though he left to go live with a girl in a different province sometime later. Rob, on the other hand, stuck it out with us for four and a half years before we let him go.

For the first few weeks we wondered about him, and politely put, Rob's a unique person. We also helped Rob get a car, which someone later stole, and is also was working for us that got Rob got his first apartment. We were paying Rob $14.50/hour when he left and even gave him some extra work with landscape installations.

It was probably a good thing that Rob left Lite-Scape and Nedco when he did because he didn't seem to like or respect his job very much. I don't want to speak poorly about him, though if you ask him, he'd probably agree that near the end, the job was not a good suit for him. I'm not sure what is.

One last note though before I pass the torch, Rob talked about you, Natalie, a bit back then, and we thought he was crazy for doing so. He needs a real girl. You know that too.

ROBERT KOYICH

WHAT DOES IT MATTER?

Natalie, I wanted to write this entire book from your perspective, though fell off course with the second and third chapters. The first chapter was an attempt to come from your perspective, the second from others, the third was intended not to be directed from myself, though beginning it, I write directly from my perspective, though not necessarily only to you.

- Spark-

Okay, I have been living in depravity. I have sometimes been thinking that I'm helpful or imperative to or for the lives of others. I have been wasting my breath away with cigarettes, I've squandered money and other resources away on myself and other people, and I have been harsh and debased with a lack of self-control. For years I have been chasing dreams that are outlandish and out of reach, and I too have been living a hedonistic lifestyle. I've tried to gain the favour of people, including yourself, and have not lived a thoroughly honourable life.

While I've learned that I should not trust some people, I too must face the consequences of my just and honest actions. Although people have told me that I should not live in fear and instead trust others, I don't always agree with that. I have been used, abused, and believe that people have betrayed me. I cannot claim to know the situation, though I thought it wasn't a good one.

My father and grandfather had advised "never lend, never borrow," and again I found myself in a situation that I had brought on myself. I'm not talking about the many thousands I owed to the bank, yet instead of the small loans to others to help them out. I seemed to think that lending money and Magic cards were a way to help, though it wrecked me again. I should have learned from the previous home never to lend people money, though my trust and faith had led me astray.

I also don't think you know you trust me. Many years ago my opinions and intents were much different. Back then I thought I 'needed' you and would be incomplete on my own. I later found that completely untrue. I can't claim even to think that it's a good idea to meet as I've been living a depraved life with little amounts of honour and respect. As I wrote in May 2013, I had the camera on my building's doors ready for an intrusion. A 'friend' I lent money to was acting very desperate, and I was in fear.

For those of you who have resources, please ensure you never front or borrow from people. If you lend, it's harder for a person to pay back a dead person, and if you borrow, some people are blood hungry to get their money back. Even though I don't do illegal drugs and am not selling them like I used to, I had again trusted someone that I should never have. If you think something or someone is a bad idea, even if you feel the twinge of un-trust, be cautious and heed your inner wisdom.

Some people say that we should trust others and be vulnerable. Is it worth sitting at home in fear that someone wants to break in your door?! Money and the want of it does strange, foul, and awful things to people. Some have called me paranoid, yet the number of times I've trusted and then been betrayed by someone wanting something I have has inclined me to think that other's shouldn't always be believed.

You too, Natalie, should know of this. How many times has somebody wanted, or even worse yet, felt entitled to have something of yours purely on the basis that they don't have what you have? If I had never blindly or foolishly trusted some people by allowing them to owe me money, I would have had a far less chance of a critical situation.

The situation, from my belief, was due to drugs and due to the person wanting them. I recall another getting pissed off at me since I didn't give them a car ride purely on the notion that I had a car and they didn't. I've been tripped up by providing some leeway and trust, to only then be sitting at home fearing the consequence of me not giving the person more.

I could go on arguing the idea of being selfless and helping anyone and everyone. Earlier in the day, I found myself saying that I want to spend my days helping people in small ways with those who'll reciprocate and help others too. In May 2013, I was wondering "Who would ever do that?!"

I've gotten pissed off and complained about small things, like people not even saying hello and going to "Do you have this or that card?" It used to happen when I had a Magic collection, and I often felt guilty for complaining about it. I was a bit ticked off that some of society has said "don't complain" when there are some definite things to complain about. Some others also know that.

When I even start to catch myself being negative or beginning to complain, I sometimes feel a twinge of guilt because of being told not to complain. For this chapter, though, I'm going to go on with "forget what society says" and get some negativity out of my system.

What is the point of me trying to help people? Note that; 'trying.' I want to help people, I don't know who to trust, and I note that way too many times I've helped people that only use and abuse. I don't want to go on about positive stories right now as it would minimize the point. I remember getting betrayed by people doing meth in my home when living in the Marlborough apartment in Vancouver.

The people stole $200 from me and got me evicted. I was foolish for letting people live in the home when I was out at work, and I also gave them my bank card. I also lent money to the people upstairs in my previous apartment to only find myself, later on, shivering in freight with the phone in hand ready to call 911.

The situation in 2013 was because I lent money to a friend and bought Magic cards and a monitor from them. Without the monitor, I wouldn't be able to write this, though I am sure as anything I could live well enough without feeling that they wanted to rob my home and hurt me.

I bought a monitor and cards from them for $200, and then, later on, they were trying to get even more money from me. I think the same person was lying to me about other stuff and I regretted ever giving them a thing. I'm just tired of people using me so much. Do I even know how to live otherwise?

Then, regarding you, there's no reason that you and I should

FRAGMENTS OF INTENT

ever even meet. I have squandered my life away on open thoughts and empty dreams, and your life is good, stable, and whole on its own. I'm just a foolish kid who fell in love in 1998 and has no idea how to get his own life on a decent track, let alone knowing how to benefit others honestly and sincerely.

You've got all you need, Natalie, and it doesn't matter what I think. My Mom is right that I've got to sort out my life, and I also note I've not done much at all to form and develop a healthy and respectful situation. I've been daftly irresponsible, have been living in filth, and no matter what anyone else says, they still don't have a clue how much I've thought or dreamt about you.

When I was in the hospital the first time in 1999, I thought you were in the delivery room birthing our twins, and at Simon Fraser University, I remember crying myself to sleep because you never phoned. I know that I obsessed and focused on you and deluded myself thinking that you were the answer to my life. When writing, I still think of our spirit and note that I apologize for soul-stalking and forcing the bond.

If there is a connection between us, it's because a drugged out kid made you the focus of his small irrational world because he was lonely and had no one else to love back then. I still want to meet, Nat, though I don't think it's a good idea to think of a relationship together.

The idea of this book was to write and invite Natalie to meet me. I've already danced with the balance and, like my life, I must repurpose this book to a different end. The slight

25

notion of getting this book complete now is just the sombre story of one kid who refuses to give up, and a message to others to bring them hope, advice, and rational thought.

The original book idea I had was '*Beautiful? Do You Mind?*' and was meant as a way for the reader to play and interact with reality. I write *this* book as a way to do something with my life. Near 14 ½ thousand words written for a romantic notion of one kid meeting his dream gal, and then the next irrational thought was still to finish the book in the chance that one person will gain value, and I don't know who they are. I hope it's not just me.

If you find yourself reading this, please know that some people do want to help and not just destroy the planet or other's lives to get what they want or think they need.

(And in 2018, I knew we are to keep finding more of them!)

When and if I meet my child, I have some ideas about how to raise him or her. One approach is to help the child grow through the first few years of life; up to the point of having a cognitive idea and impression of self. I'd like to have a daughter named Aeris. The name is from Final Fantasy VII for if and when my gal and I settle down and have a child.

Rules, I think, are fundamental, though they should hopefully not be so limiting. The premise of an idea is to form guidelines with my child. The plans I have for Aeris are, at this point, few, and rules are part of it. What I want to do is form rules *with* Aeris.

When Aeris is old enough to talk and think with others, I want to start a book and list rules that she, her Mom, and I create. I want Aeris to help form these rules so that she knows, understands and accepts them. In the beginning, some might be simple yet essential. I want Aeris to shape her behaviours to be acceptable in her own eyes, and not just our family's.

I don't like telling people what to do, and I also value self-accountability. By Aeris agreeing on rules, consequences will be known and set with and *by* her and not just *for* her. Some parents make all the rules, and sometimes the kids don't like those rules. If Aeris understands and forms the rules that she agrees to abide by, it keeps her part of the equation and will encourage self-responsibility.

I want to journal the process of living with my children. I had started a journal two years ago with the intent to give the journal to my wife when we got married. That notebook has since fizzled since the one that I was forming that book for was a gal I worked with at Wendy's. I had a dream to hook up with her and go to the 2014 Olympics and conceive a child in Sochi. The plan didn't go through, though, as she rejected me and we never formed a relationship.

I've had many dreams that have fizzled, and I blame myself since I've been told we shape, mould, and develop our lives. During Christmas 2010-2011, I wandered around Darling Harbor in Sydney, Australia anticipating a meeting with Natalie. During other Christmas' I've been convinced that a meeting with Natalie was inevitable to happen Christmas morning. I've been a delusional fool for most of my life, and it goes back to how I still seem to go on waiting for my life to happen without seeding a full and proper amount of effort.

When I was 15 years old, I got my first job (other than flyers and papers) at Wendy's, and I kept that job full through high-school. I had a car, I had some friends, and I could do most anything. We'd go to play laser tag at Laser Quest, hang out at friend's homes, or play video games like Super Nintendo or Sega Genesis. Those times were great times in my life.

I remember 2002 when I moved to Chilliwack. For two and a half years, I lived in a group home where I had so few responsibilities. We had $85 spending money a month, though had all food, shelter, and bills covered. It's almost like my glory days. Dan D, Cory B, and Craig L were my best friends, and it was great fun. We'd go fishing at Island 22 or swimming in the gravel pond and drink Cokes and smoked, talked, and joked on the patios.

When I moved out of the group home, I was in the music making mode. I recorded and produced songs, I had a job at a mushroom barn, and I had my two cats. Within a year of leaving the group home, I gained my post with a warehouse. I kept that job for almost four years and was earning $2000 or so after taxes a month. In April 2009 I was let go. I got a job (again) with Wendy's in June 2009 and worked there for three years. Two stints at a call centre and six months as a dishwasher later found me writing this book.

I believe I do have value, though if I think I can help someone, people may view it as me as acting like I'm in a higher position than another. Something I read is the statement: "Everyone is our superior in one way or another." I'm inclined to list off a bunch of people and how they're my superior, though add the idea of God as being the ultimate superior.

FRAGMENTS OF INTENT

There's the intrinsic value of noble intent, though that doesn't always mean a good result will occur. But calling my intentions 'noble' has an arrogant tone to it too. I want to live, love, and thrive, though the lyrics drive forward that I've heard. The words on the page note that some want to rip me out like a sprout from the soil.

Some may try to boil the blood while others may want me to hit the ground with a solid thud. Mindsound is not a bright bud because of the ways I light people and seem to chew my cud continually. The irony is my Magic Cards were in the bank and not in the mess of my home, though they say: "when in Rome." Here I am and not there like a gem as the hem of the patchwork quilt helps tilt the machine. It lets the sounds be keen to radiate from this side of heaven's gate.

I find that there is value in what we do and that I must wait and curate the flow. I seem to deem many know the things that I do without having to push it onto us. The bus guides the forces of the courses of how they will be now while a farmer uses Oxen to pull ahead plow. Now the Tao, and somehow, cow, cast the wares we sell to let the correct mix of my soul, spirit, and heart meld and gel.

Some tell the story of how the quarries we find lined players and prayers entwined like Tooth and Nail. We bring my lovestone and Aeris to the pale facts of how the tracts I've seen find that I do shed my fear and sin. Friends become keen like kin, and as we're living, I'm glad for it to win.

And then an irresponsible choice made at 2:01 AM on June 26th, 2013. At that point, I needed to sleep to wake up and get a real job. Instead, I found myself on the computer writing again. I'd used Kevin as an excuse to stay up late and also wanted to sleep to be responsible and search for work the next day.

I found that I was exhausted and tired and wanting to stay awake all night with the irrelevant idea of writing. Even though my Dad has said to never think of Natalie, she is a dear lovestone. I don't know who the real Natalie is or how she and I can ever meet. I don't want to label her as *my* lovestone as I don't know her, and Natalie is a person far out of my league. No one will ever own her; she is her own woman.

It's a tear of wanting to do something with my life and the creative process of writing for someone I've never known. My keys push past the point of writing rhymes, and I could have climbed into bed for sleep. I'm exhausted for not yet knowing my gal, I'm without my cats, and I'm without a life that I would be glad and proud to promote and share.

Still, this is where we live.

FROM THE SOUL TO SPIRIT

Our future, we hear it well on both sides of the Shell. One full well higher than Heaven, and the other to save us from Hell. I had forgotten your soul, yet I had heard your voice. I thought you knew who I was, and even though we'd not yet met, I have made choices in life. If I accidentally rip up some good seed when I weed the soil, I think of how Judy had said I didn't torch the fields as I thought I had.

August 3rd, 2013. I left my job as a dishwasher at Bozzini's. There was love, angst, and a lack of self-control. I also understood that I'd not yet known my role. I won't cast myself a spade, though I wade in the drink of how my tantrums are in the link. You hated the anger with a passion, and though my love can hone in on the issues, we found the tears shed without tissues. The mascara drips slow down the cheek, and even if we do get the chance to speak, I expect you already know who I am.

There's no way to understand the sorrow I felt. It was not woe, though, as that's deeper in the future. Yes, I have cried many tears, and I've also thought she was rolling her eyes at me. The many dreams of meeting are a kind reminder of being held in another's arms. I've not tended so well to the idea of meeting, though I thought of the lyric "something tells me it's a marriage made in heaven." I'm worthy and capable of love now, though am still sometimes surprised when it happens.

There were many years when I had no love or respect, just the desire to get what I want. Now I'm starting to love and appreciate people and let them know I do. I learn to honour others and have developed a reverence for the value of life. For many years I had disliked some of the things that people do, and know I'm capable of hate. I wish not to feel that. I'll write more from other people's perspective as I learn how to understand them. I do love, and Nat cannot be the only one that I do.

When I was in the UBC hospital, there was a heart drawn on the smoke room wall that said 'Love just me, and Enguleena too.' Elizabeth told me that Lori wrote it, and I believed Lori was Natalie and that Enguleena was the name of our future daughter. I revoked love from all others because of my obsession. Enchantments can hold firm and aren't easily removed.

I love my parents, and I have learned to like some things about myself. I too have found that, for some people, I can say "I love you" and mean it. I made a terrible choice the previous night to quit my job. It may mean that I messed up my life, though I'm glad to be here at home. I need to build my future, and I will need a lot of support from others. I also note I'm ready and willing to till fields of good seed, even if we may not yet harvest them.

I am a child.

I am a soul.

I do love.

FRAGMENTS OF INTENT

I also know I'm poor when I wrote this.

Breathe in, and breathe out.

I took a course called *Phase One* at PD Seminars two different times. There was a day during the program called *Shadow Day* where we went on a meditation into our deepest fears. The first time I took the course, I nearly met that situation. I'm only now understanding the idea from the second time I took the program.

During the first time I took the course, the situation I found myself within my mind was being killed in a forest by three people. That nearly happened. I got jacked three times by the same three people at two different locations. Two of the three wanted to take me to the ravine and kill me, while one of them I had known indirectly in High School. I mentioned a name of a friend to one of them, and though I refer to the friend's name in a recording I made, it was the leader of the trio who saved me by not giving the order to kill me. I thank them and wish peace and love may keep them safe too.

The second time I was in Phase One, I found myself thinking of Natalie and found brambles preventing me from getting to her. There is and were many barriers that I need to pass if I'm to meet her. Even if I don't have complete faith or an idea how to:

There is a future for me.

There too is a future for you.

I'll keep on dreaming as my aunt Norma's birthday card said to do. I know I want to meet her, though don't know how.

33

Selfishly, this book is all about me. It's to let you know who I am, where I come from, and what I have been through. If you ever read this book, you have given me a great gift. I thank you no matter if it's understood or not, and note that even if it isn't, it's a way of me sharing the view from True. There are many that I do and shall love; the fact is Natalie's the one who's had the most substantial impact on my soul.

When I left my job at Bozzini's, I thought I would come home and write you my plan for the next few months. That didn't happen. Instead, now, I find myself writing with no secure idea or plan as to how to let these words reach your eyes. I'm just glad that I know who I'm writing to and that we can have this. Thank you very much for being part of my life, even if we've never met. Does this make Natalie just my muse?

"It takes two to write, and one to read."

I also don't want to creep you out. That is a significant issue. If you have no idea who I am and have never heard my heart or my voice, then I'm just another that seems to think I've had a deep connection. I don't doubt that I would like Natalie, though I also think the way I meet her is to connect with you through writing and have her find me.

The main point I want to make of life, mine, yours, or anyone's, is to do what we like to do and also to find a way to support ourselves to do so. I found that my dreams continue to change and there's the fact I like writing. It's also correct writing can't yet support me financially. What I'm trying to do is figure out what I would like to do with and for the rest of my life, and though I believe writing is a significant part of

FRAGMENTS OF INTENT

that, I also want to clarify how I'll meet my future family; including Mom and Dad when they're 90 years old.

The Glass House is a vision. It's a home I designed and visualize, and I'm wondering about the hows, whys, and when. I'm solo right now, and, no, I don't entirely know how I'll be able to afford the home. I want to take care of Mom and Dad when they get older, and I don't have a blue clue who I should be writing to sometimes. It's kind of funny and harsh how the Chilliwack part of The Contialis seems to ream out of my mind and into my ears with their judgments and opinions.

Then a conversation switches the stance and not the blade. Made to fit no particular category, the story chips away at the quarry with a trip to Lori. I found people pillaging my mind and being unkind. A few choice words lined get them out of the way so we may pray with people who understand the depths of what I say.

While I could write about the nights I cried, I too correlate that I'm fearful of heaven's gate. When I get the people to say and create, the laughter of some seems to betray an eight. There are the thoughts they want me to have, and even though the flow is sometimes what we wind, I don't like it when people till seeds for us to be unkind. Now that I can write without the sprouts torn from the soil, it's true you mentioned that the blood does boil. The plow now suggests some gals and what I like about them.

I like Felicia because she is positive. She also loves life and other animals. I enjoy some of the gals at Starbucks because they smile and have fun. I like Jenn Steadman a lot because she invites herself over and is a friend in the loop with the jokes. Jenn Miller is radically cool because she let me talk to her and let me read some of this book out loud to her at Clouda's before the shop closed.

I love Mom because although she nudges me along with the job search, she also wants me to thrive. I think she knows that although I've not put full effort into finding work, she wants me to prosper and knows I'm not like the usual parts of the human population. I like my Dad's wife Sarah because she has helped support me and keeps cool with Dad. I love Julianna because of her positivity and her devotion to her kids.

It's tricky with the world always on my brain and watching my situation. It seems I can't make choices without a slew of people knowing I go off topic and get critical. It's because I think some people, like me, aren't following the proper actions. We've been told not to judge, and then criticize every decision another makes. We've been told to think for ourselves, then we drain the mind of another.

When others latch onto my being tilling seeds for security and defence, it's a devious situation. It was difficult for me to not be angry at them for messing with my mind and body. What, though, is the benefit of me running away from situations and the repressed memories? Because they couldn't control a unique position, let's go further back to the beginning of this.

The first point of meeting Natalie and her music was in December 1997. I was on a flight to Australia to visit my Dad and Sarah on CP Air. I saw Natalie on the monitor with her video for Torn, and she fascinated me. I remember

FRAGMENTS OF INTENT

seeing her get kissed at the end of the video and it was quite heartbreaking. I don't have a memory of the actual syntactic thoughts I had, though I seem to think that it was love at first sight. Even though I may have seen Natalie on Neighbors, the Australian drama, her playing Beth was a memory that may have zapped out of me (I went through electroshock therapy).

I have a memory of my Dad and I driving in a green convertible when we were in Sydney and hearing Torn again. Many years later I still hear that song creep into my awareness. At Walmart, I was outside having a ciggie and was thinking about Nat, and when I got back in the store, I heard the end of the song. The song has morphed a lot through the years; sometimes the lyrics sound just a bit different. Though she doesn't know how much I had cried, since she's never yet met me, we know that I haven't shown her how to cry. It's something I barely ever do anymore.

Summer 1998 (North America) found my Mom and I meeting up with Katie and Lori Scozzafava when I finally found the CD *Left of the Middle*. I can see the shop in mind when I saw the picture on the front cover. Again, with a Louis CK reference, if chicken wings are amazing, then there is no adequate word to describe how and what I've thought of her at that time. I loved her. I missed her. I also note, when written, she's not ever one that was *'Wishing I Was There.'*

During summer 1998, I was in a clinical depression; I felt buckets of sadness and also cried a lot. From the line in the album *Left of the Middle* "I'm pushing zero… where is my hero" I used to pray that Natalie was pressing the zero on the phone to call me. I would mentally call out my phone number hoping and praying with my entire being for her to call me. I would cry when I didn't receive a phone call from her back then when I was obsessed.

I played *Left of the Middle* full through every night for about three months. I remember singing the entire album into the reflection in the computer monitor while a candlelit face called to me in the dark room. I saw what I thought was Natalie's face in the screen a lot during that play of the album. It was like her soul was calling out to me through the reflection. A lot of lyrical morphs happened during that play.

I sometimes hear different lyrics, even now a bit. Is it 'the pigeons and the crumbs' or 'pigeons and the crows'? The words I hear from the album are not the same as in the liner notes, though that too delves into nodal music theory; a theory that different people will listen to different lyrics from the same recording. Music is often guided by *who* is listening, playing, or owning the music.

I made it through summer 1998 at Louis Riel House on SFU campus. It's a place I would like to go again and take my gal to see the lights of Vancouver at night. There were a few holy places for me at SFU. The grass pyramid was another place other than the Louis Riel roof, and on the path to Burnaby Mountain Park, below the townhouses, there was a trail and spot where I found the Metamorphic Heart.

The Metamorphic Heart is a heart-shaped stone I found in a stone circle that someone had cast. I shouldn't have broken the ring, though the rock became a significant part of my spiritual wanderings. The stone was given to my Mom many years later, and from what I'm aware, I lost the rock to the sands of time. The stone had a corner broken off of it that represented Thea, the Original Lovestone, while the remainder of the stone signified Natalie.

I fell for Thea before Natalie, and wonder if it was Thea who cast the circle. She was Wiccan, and it may have been her. At the same place where I had broken the ring, I built a stone model of BC (including a hidden pool table) and spent much time there. I called that place The Lovestone City and wrote a lot of poetry and lyrics there. I had a spot a meter or two up the path that was my own bleakly cared for garden that I called the Lovestone Park. Others intermittently used the route as I sat and played at the city and park.

Part of what I would like to acknowledge is that my being has travelled through much time and experience since then. Although in theory, I'm the same person from when I was born until now, I'm not sufficiently confident that I can believe that. If time *is* entirely linear, it's true that we are *all* on the same timeline. We each have travelled through space, time, and experience, yet also all theoretically have existed along the same corresponding dimension of time. If each year that passes is directly linear, from the point of our birth until now, and even further into the future, we move together.

If it's the same timeline and sequence of moments, though, it's crazy to think that we've all been on this planet for so long. Even if that awareness is only from feeling it's seemed like eons since I lived as a 5-year-old child, I'm not sure what my intents are now for this section, so shall carry on to the next.

ROBERT KOYICH

WHAT WERE YOU DOING, ROBERT?

Okay, so this chapter is intended to describe how I'd been living through the few months before June 2014. I had run Koyich Digital as a company for January through May 2014 selling Magic cards I had bought. The sales of the cards were to support Koyich Digital and me until the music set off. The case of the matter, though, is that the company caused far too many issues communally. There also was an issue of refuelling inventory and that the Magic card sales were not profitable enough to support the company.

The music hadn't sold so much up to then either, and I note if the music does go off, I can claim part of that money as personal funds. I don't need a company to track the music, though did get wholly invested in tracking inventory and expenses with the Magic. I liked running the company for the brief time it was legally bound, and note the accounting course I took at university was helpful. The dissolution of the company was officially May 13th, 2014.

My actual day to day activities hadn't varied much. I attended Bastion Games, a local card shop, for Magic and communal contacts, I was partly involved in church, and I also had written many rhymes, pages, and parts of my books when sitting at Starbucks.

My sleep was not structured well. Some nights I stayed up all night working on the computer to give Kevin car rides at 5 AM. Sometimes friends visited my place; groups of four to six, and at other times just one friend to interact with through the late nights. My ideal sleep schedule was to stay awake until I was tired, no matter what time it is, and sleep until I eventually wanted to rise. I.e. to stay up as late as I want and rest until entirely reset.

I needed to find a job and scanning the internet and applying online wasn't enough of an effort to finding work. Ideally, I'd love to earn my money writing on the computer for other people, though I had barely any audience and almost zero demand for my writing at that point. I'd like to remember to write pages of flowetics for people, though deem that I have some other good ideas for people to help build their lives. I'd love to be a life coach, though hadn't taken steps to be one. That's later in the process.

I liked helping people with cards and car rides. Again, I love helping some people, though my primary issue has been a lack of income. I want to earn my money and generate a reliable income that is greater than my expenses. In June 2014, I was on $905 PWD (disability) per month with a great deal more than that spent each month. That's how I accumulated the substantial debt I mentioned earlier in the book.

I got an electronic cigarette which had reduced my smoking from one and a half to two packs of cigarettes per day to less than one. I like and love coffee and visit Starbucks often, and I work on my computer there. I had written many personal pages and more than half of *Finding Natalie* at Starbucks. Sometimes I've gotten agitated by some of the contialitic/shoulic things and people at the shops, though I prefer being out of my apartment to write sometimes.

FRAGMENTS OF INTENT

I wanted to start typing my dreams, goals, and visions into this chapter. I have been told by others (family, friends, and society) that I need to have a job to support myself. I deem that to be true, partly. The post I wish to have is more diverse and not a standard hourly position. I'd love to form an income through creating and supporting futures and the lives of others and myself instead.

The rhyming, writing, and recording of lyrics have made a lot of material, though I've not put the work into marketing effectively. I'd been more of a persistent novelty act, though through 2014 I had 2,107 plays of my tracks on Koyich Digital's Bandcamp page. Another primary thing I gleaned from running Koyich Digital was a batch of printed demo discs I distributed.

The Glass House is a home I've designed in my mind and where I want to live in 2025. I can easily visualize the interior of the home; it's a vision, not a dream. The house will be located in Chilliwack or Australia, though the image I see of it shifts between Chilliwack and Australia. The central area of the home is 'the pit' which is a sitting area lowered from the main floor of the home. I can see my child's room, and it's a room that I'd love to have. There isn't much outdoor space, though there's an area for a table outside on the right-hand side of the home and a small patio at the back of the house too. I have no idea yet with whom I'll live within this home, though having the vision in mind allows me to work towards it.

When it comes to who I'll live with, I think of my girlfriend situation. I've only had two or three girlfriends in Chilliwack, and the 'Natalie Dream' was a major issue with each. It reminded me of how when I started writing this book a long time ago (2013) that I focused heavily on the dream. Now, in 2017 and 2018, I've lightened up on the pressure, and I'm not certain it's a good idea.

There are a few gals that I like or love, though I can't foresee them in the Glass House. I love Jenn, though know she and I shouldn't meld considering a few things. In 2017 she got engaged, so that removed any potential relationship, though I liked her a lot. I prefer to meet my gal and form life, and hopefully child, with the starting point of just her and I. I'd like to adopt a cat again and note that the one I wanted to select is named Belle. Belle was a dearly beautiful calico at the Chilliwack Animal Safe Haven, though was adopted in 2015.

Over time we can tell I'm focusing more on how and what I want without thinking so much of Natalie. I'd like to hook up with a real gal, and in 2018 meeting Natalie is not the goal that it used to be when I first wrote this book. In 2018 the idea to meet Natalie seems like a long obsessed point of never knowing that higher powers of life control with the primary objective to thrive. We shall.

My parents are very rational, practical, supportive, and forgiving parents, and they don't advocate for Natalie. They have both pushed for me to have a primary job to support my life. I worked fast food or restaurant jobs though they jeopardized my mental stability and sanity each time I've worked them. Working at the local call centre isn't an option, and I applied to all the leading grocery stores in town. I worked warehousing from 2005 to 2009 though hold a tainted remembrance of my experience.

FRAGMENTS OF INTENT

I'm not okay to have to work a job of which I'll turn to hate, get fired, or have to quit again. It may be that I'm an idealist or foolish, though I tend to think I manifest a brilliant life, pay my debts, and earn my home. For now, I'm happy to live in my apartment, and with enough heart, love, and care, I receive and keep myself afloat, I swim back to shore with enough time, effort, and energy.

I'm okay to live where I am for another five to seven years; that's an asset too. I won't need to move from the apartment I live in and then turn back to my fear of pushing forward without having yet achieved great success. I wanted to adopt Belle and want to have a job so that I can afford to have a car again. I think a life of loving a pet and finding a real gal in Chilliwack is in line with my core values and will be a life I am allowed to enjoy thoroughly.

A primary concern I have is how I'll find my gal. For more than a decade I'd been fixated on 'finding Natalie' and note that it's almost like I don't want to give up the dream. The irrational thought is deeming the decades or pining for her are a waste if I don't get to meet her. I've also turned my hopes and dreams and heart towards producing and providing the next generations.

In 2014 I had purchased two long-term investments and gifts for two of my nieces. I bought Hope a Mox Pearl for $575 and a Mox Ruby for Mackenzie for $700. The cards now are worth far more than what I paid for them, though I sold them both to cover a mortgage payment. There was a concern that Magic cards might not hold the same monetary value many years later, yet as of June 2018, I didn't own any Magic cards. I sold them all.

My situation in 2014 had $6,000 available for supporting myself, though that available money was credit money and not savings. Since I lost my job with Nedco and Lite-Scape, the warehousing job, I relied heavily on a line of credit to keep myself afloat. With many irresponsible purchases, bankruptcy was inevitable for me. For now, I'll finish this chapter and seed the future weeks. I get to travel to Edmonton and plan on cleaning and organize the home in which I live.

There are many people with whom I interact with; some I like and love and still forget about them so often. There are fewer users in my life now, and some friends again can visit my home. I'm glad when they do. I continue developing my life and planting the right seeds for future yields, and when the rhymes are peeled away from the nights in the day, we shall find that my daughter too will learn, love, live, thrive, create, play and pray.

Though they may try to take my dreams away, I note that some things will live forever and a day. Please guard, treasure, and foster your soul and stay in connection with the people that you like and love. You do matter, and though there are some who may want to use and abuse, do not be afraid to limit their involvement in your life. Although some of us yet have to have met our wants and needs, God helps us tend the fields and gardens and helps us keep and till the seeds.

RITE FROM THE SPRITE

What's up Sapphire!? Remember not to wear your sunglasses and to let your brilliant eyes shine bright! You knew well what the situation was and meld the spelled Id to find that I hid a past bid of one who already has a kid. Through the bits made to byte, a sprite helped let me wade in the games we've played. The fact too is that Emerald may view how you partly know what it is to be Blu. For those who don't know who I'm referring to, the facts of the book haven't yet been shown to be true.

I removed the previous chapter of this book. I wrote it to a friend codenamed Chandra as she was the real girl in the real girl/dream girl dilemma. It had been one month since I gave her some questions to answer and we'd not had a relationship talk recently. She hadn't yet answered some significant and essential questions I asked, and we were in a holding pattern. It was a bit comforting, yet disturbing, floating without knowing what the truth is. I'd not been seeking many goals or dreams, and I've wanted to have and form some good source of purpose.

I like giving people car rides and other things, though the Natalie dream also is one I value because of who I need to become, and what I will need to do, to 'achieve' the goal. I put the word achieve in quotes because I know meeting Natalie is not just an objective to accomplish and then drop. A notion of meeting her includes "if I meet her, what then?"

If this book is meant to form the story of how I meet my gal, and also help us process and clarify my wants, may it assist other ideas too? With some of the mental energies and thoughts, it shows I want to be closer to my Dad. Some of my friends have lost their Dads, and some other friends have different relationships with their Dads. One friend dislikes their father, and the other also does, though has never known his. Anita and I hold a different situation as we both know our Dads are and loved, though differently as her Dad passed on. After knowing Anita for about a year, I knew that she loved her Dad dearly and adored him in a similar sense than I mine. I wish her Dad were still here.

I love my Dad dearly. He is a man who has sacrificed so much and also demonstrates love and kindness to me. Even though my Mom raised me from grade seven on, my Dad now is one of the people on this planet that I adore, love, cherish, and trust the most. I've learned to love and respect my Mom more, though when growing up, she and I would argue a lot.

My Mom and my Dad split when the three of us lived in Hong Kong. For a few years after that, I was angry at my Dad. I took him leaving as that he loved my step-mum more than my Mom and I combined. It's been 25 years plus, and though I accept my situation and like how my Dad and I have developed, my parents' divorce affected me severely. Even if my Dad wasn't living in the same country as me from grade seven onwards, he did help raise me. He is exceptionally supportive of me and is one of the most important people in my life.

I also wonder, rewinding to the beginning of this book, what is the intent now that I've not been so focused on Natalie? I've used this book to explain and share the journey towards finding my gal and still don't think that one specific lovestone should be written off. I've felt that she's held me away from other gals and playing me like a riddle for her situation. There have been times where she seems to be utterly false, and at other times she shows herself as being remarkably true.

Chandra is, and hopefully always will be, a friend, though I think of how she gives me hugs. They don't feel like love. Maybe that's a sign. Anita gave me a wonderful hug the day I gave her the first chapters of this book and hugs remind me who is a true friend. Maybe I'm judgmental about how people are with physical contact. Physical touch is one of my best ways to show love, though some people may not share the love in the same way.

There are defence and safety in not being hooked up and held in a relationship. The idea that lingers is, partly, that the people of Chilliwack know this entire play and that they're playing me like a game. I don't like that. It also inclines me to delude myself by considering people are playing a part and role in a conspiracy. The previous places I've lived also showed their plots and plans, and it comes down to the fact that I honestly don't know who to trust.

I don't want to slander, though I don't think she loves me as a mate. Secondarily, I believe that seducing me could be a trap. If I hold my focal and potentially paranoid delusions, corruption of my heart and falling into lust could ruin myself if I fall into temptation. Then again, Karen of Esso recommended I try a real relationship and learn from it to use in the future. One friend told me to 'just go for it' with

Chandra, though I didn't think it a good idea.

So now, a moment to assess my current situation. I draw a breath to find where I am, where I want to go, what I want to do, and why I want to do it.

I thrive, I keep ploughing communal fields with good seed, and I'll heed the intuition I receive. I'm still very much a present based entity and haven't planned well. I'm was without a job or paid employment, though I didn't think others are okay with that. I may be okay, though as needed and required, I can focus on writing again.

I see the Glass House. I know that to build that home I'll need to save and earn a lot of money. I don't know how to generate income from the recordings made and don't want to use so much push marketing. I want to help bridge connections, people, and friends and introduce others. I teach others and build more relationships within our community, and though I want to be community support, I'm a bit limited by having few friends and contacts. I adjust that fact and how I behave.

I know I have a good, kind, and sometimes meek, heart. I also know I have a damaging potential to be extreme on the opposite side of the spectrum. When I was forming parts of this book, I was cursing vigorously about the technology freezing while I attempted to work. If I chose to abide by my prerogatives, assure I'm working to be a plus one and not a negative one, my decisions still may need adjustment.

I'm sometimes concerned with how delicate and daft I can be in my stubbornness. I've not always accepted fact and reality. Our environment has a significant effect on people; like how the music I hear allows me to feel hopeful. I remind myself of the fact I'm working for peace, and I need to reset and gather, and then regather, myself so often. Writing is a way that helps me to do so.

My cousin Julianna gave me a notebook one time that pretty well reminds me that I need to write to stay alive.

"A layer of light, luck, life, and love from above to guard you and keep you like a peaceful dove."

Remember when I call someone a Sapphire, it can mean that they are vocal or verbose. Sapphires are often genuine, though a base idea is the symbol of blue mana is a water drop. Sapphires can shed tears, and I know there is no other way to label some with Magic or Shoulspeak. A lovestone knows I have the capacity of sadness, and also anger and love.

Sprite, I note that with friends, you're sensitive to how others affect you. You remind me that friends should be tended to, and there are love and likeness between some people that we're not in direct relationship with at this point. You also remind me that friends are an essential thing in life and that even when we've not spoken with a friend for a very long time, that it doesn't mean they're not a friend.

Some we haven't spoken or met for a long time, though they make our heart smile. I'm glad you're a friend that I don't *need* to talk to so often. We know we like and have a form of love between us, and with the animal topic, it shows a great sign about how our pets respond. "If my dog doesn't trust you, I shouldn't either." This saying may mean that some should be cautious of others because of how their dogs respond. I also think of how the way other friend's pets treat me to show that I am a friend and trustworthy.

I love meeting friend's pets. I also like meeting other people's parents sometimes. I know it's a very telling sign of how we are. With such a capacity for love and compassion, we get pissed off at the right things, and we love animals to show a significant element of our heart. Some of the love you have for friends also shows how even when people are mean to us or mistreat us, that we keep our love and likeness. Compassion shows how you do have a fantastic capacity to love too!

The downside of having a beautiful heart, though, is when you like or love someone and the relationship doesn't form. I thought of writing to a different friend later in this book, though the way that others have been friends also shows me my obsessions aren't healthy. One friend kept on about another, and even when the other said 'no' and shut out the friend, they still tried to force the relationship.

With Natalie and me, there is no way of her rejecting me and telling me "no" to my face. There is a notion of safety knowing she can't refuse me, yet I need to release the dream. The lingering hope was what pulled me forward for years. I went for Natalie, even though I've never yet known who she is in real life.

The link word is 'obsession,' though. The difference is the world is telling me to _not_ go for Natalie the way I was telling a friend to not go for the other. No matter how much I tried to tell the friend to 'let it go,' she generally didn't. So many times I've been told to give up the dream or to 'let it go' and often told people that I couldn't; that it was just a part of my heart. "Tell blue not to be blue" I would say.

Sapphire believed that she could force the connection, and we know it couldn't form. I seemed to think I could meet Natalie, and we know now that I want to respond differently. The Natalie dream is a trap. I had fallen into the pit, and I feel awful about it. It doesn't seem fair to trap ourselves in loving someone when they're not able or wanting to reciprocate. The friend's crush said no, and Natalie has never had the chance to speak to me.

It's quite depressing and negative for me to think or write about Natalie. It reminds me of my Feb 2nd, 2015 challenge to Jeff Probst. I messaged every day for a week and didn't get a response. False hope is what I don't like. I don't know how I would respond if I were just told 'no.' Maybe I refuse and give up way too soon. It's like the opposites of 'forget it, it will never happen' to 'well if I don't know it's not going to happen, I would at least like a direct response.' It's a total flustercluck.

So what should I do!? From 2015, I found that Chandra and I are a no go. I'm single with no dangling potentials, and I'm not sure if I'm okay with that. The dilemma is almost a real girl/no girl argument, and now it's kind of nice to know I'm not actually in a relationship. I don't know who and what I'm searching for now. Solo at the Starbucks again is saddening and depressing, though I laugh it off because I want to remain glad. I take a breath and know that if I keep spinning my wheels, I could fall back to the similar spots and notions.

I'm inclined to write of how I value freedom so highly that

maybe I'm terrified of being locked in a relationship. That's not entirely accurate because I've envisioned a life path. I can use so many words to describe the same things from many different perspectives, yet is it retracing, or replacing?

It's challenging to build a life as one, and that's where friends help a lot for me. Talking and processing, understanding advice and recommendations, and learning different perspectives also help guide me. I work solo a lot, though one thing of Chandra is that she didn't give input or advice or share a vision. It was me dreaming and wishing about the life her and I were to live. I could see a life a decade from now, she could not, and shared experience is best when built *together*; not one for another.

Where am I going to find a gal with whom to build? Probably not writing at the Starbucks in another solo activity. Anyhow, as this chapter and the others show, I'm a mix of everything and nothing. I hold many issues that claw at my soul that seem to be the same ones that have been haunting me for decades. Another good question: Why would any gal ever want to hook up with me anyways?

Perchance I should ship off to the next chapter. I hadn't an idea yet who I'd write to in that chapter or if I'd write from someone else's perspective. My life is an elective in which I wish to earn, learn, live, and give and I still hadn't an idea what the universe shall help me build. I mix in how these words and pages are still mentally and conscio-accidentally spilled into how we all know; I may no-go a show to find and meet the lovestone for which I'm to help learn, develop, and grow.

A FRAGMENT OF INTENT

You closed the doors. This day is another for you to do what you do to grow, nurture, and develop. The idea of one 'closing a chapter' of their life is accurate. The impression I had, though, was to close the book on Natalie.

Be free! Be you!! Because you are the one to form and forge your fate!

Natalie, or rather the dream of her is closed. Thrive! Even if I think a decade or more of her was too much, it brought me forward and taught me many lessons. We overcome the hurdle of living explicitly for another without reciprocation.

Think of how you closed some other people out of your life. You chose to abide by your prerogatives, as have I; to learn, to love, to live, to thrive, and to create.

This book, even if not to reach the hands of the one for whom it started, can be read and kept to share our journey. I'll continue writing, recording, and reciting, yet never give up on the chance to, as Mom said, err on the side of what is good.

Even if you now accept Natalie as being a false hope or dream, remember with this chapter and book that you helped me learn to look within. You know I don't *need* Natalie the way I thought I had. At one point in my life, I felt I needed to meet Natalie to complete my life. I loved her, though now know I must be free by myself to abide. The fact is she impacted my heart through the decades before the birth of our child.

Write a new book, or track it as a life journal to share. You haven't given up on the Glass House, you haven't stopped writing or recording, and you've learned to give and share. Don't allow yourself to put yourself into situations you wish not to be. Form your life with the will of God, who you are, and who you can be.

Each day, I ask you to renew your mind, connections, and spirit. Your soul is a good one, and you will carry on with life to further develop your heart. Do not have it chained. I write to remind you of a few things that you've yet to understand.

Your life *is* yours, *and* it includes many more than a few. You know that *The QBlue Project* is now meant to explain what you have formed. The goal is no longer to meet Natalie. The goal is to learn and develop and create for people *and* to earn, acquire, improve, and ensure you work well on your dreams.

What are your dreams? Your dreams may be to thrive and reach the point of seeing clearly that you need not have another to complete you; that you are whole on your own. The people you allow in your life should be ones that you want in your life, and be sure you honour them; be sure you love them. Be confident you will treasure them and help them be glad by forming a life that is right, noble, full, and pure.

Just like anyone else, there will ever only be one of you.

I thank you for being one to remember others and the

FRAGMENTS OF INTENT

lessons they and you teach. Although you reached out so many times to so many people, that too may have been the right idea. Be more conscious of what you want in your life. Choose what you will allow, and not allow. Remember that your choices will form the results you seek.

You learn.

You love.

You live.

You thrive.

You create.

Keep the sands of sleep deep in tears you shed. Note, forever, that by the entire contialis you're led. You hold a heart that has a capacity way beyond your understanding, and it is for many more than a few, not just the one you selected.

I am a person who knows I haven't figured out all the details, though I also know you hold the bold dream of not letting anything stop us from creating a life for which we love. I'm aware you may be afraid of not knowing what to do, though the things you'll need to understand are kept for what you know and knew.

ROBERT KOYICH

WHAT WOULD YOU LIKE TO KNOW?

The first book started with an audience of one, Natalie. The intent I held when I wrote the introduction and first chapter of *Finding Natalie* was to write an entire book from her perspective. I wanted to write the book as if I was her, and still be entirely truthful, to show her I understood her. I thought that if I could write an entire book from her perspective, that it would be 'proof' that I knew enough about her for her to make an effort to meet. I wanted to prove myself to Natalie, and lure her in from my understanding of her.

I still don't know who she is, yet as the movie *Dogma* said: *"I have an idea."*

My ability to write to people has improved over the years. I still see myself as a writer more than an artist, though I've given myself a few different job titles and roles. They keep me from narrowing down the view of myself. I'm not trapped or locked in a specific title, position, or function, though I work as a Contialitic Shoulsman. I also am responsible for learning and sharing truth and must keep some secrets safe. I shall.

A Facebook friend tended to me and my work by recommending a book titled *I Could Do Anything I Want to Do: If Only I Knew What it Was* by Barbara Sher with Barbara Smith. It's a great book recommendation. I learned a lot from the book and found a great deal of insight into myself, my profession, and my ideas for vocation. I also learned about my control dramas and gleaned insight into how others have helped form me into who I am.

There are many influences I've received and heeded, and though I may chatter on about different things and can babble nonsense or random to people, there are many things that I share that are not random. Different people hold different interests and also receive information from multiple channels. The values that people hold vary in that some things that matter so much to some people, yet may be like dirt to another. An idea with me, though, is that what another holds as dirt may spin into my clouds.

Gary Vaynerchuk is one that speaks of how we should hold explicit awareness and knowledge of what matters the most to ourselves, our wants, and our dreams. He tells us then to go out and earn them. That's what I want to do and shall continue to do. I also wonder about some of you, and why you can't seem to see I slant the view from the mountaintop alluding to how I too am learning when to slow or stop.

There are many layers of and through this planet, and it's also the fact that although theoretically, we are all on the same Earth. Each of our lives is sometimes in different worlds with thoroughly different parameters. If I'm to be self-aware and even find a global story to unfold, it also will require me to understand these different lives and settings. I must know how we overlap, connect, and interact, though the thread winding this dream into the timeline of Earth also finds me not to get too predictive. What will happen?

I still don't know.

FRAGMENTS OF INTENT

What I think I need to understand, cultivate, and develop is that life is the primary value. Some people yearn to help others achieve their dreams, and I'm one of those people. I too am a bit overly money focused for my liking. I have strong hopes, goals, ideas, and also ethics, yet I too am still learning my value proposition to earn the results of my beings desire; to be self-sufficient and work into the future with enough to not just survive, yet to thrive!

Knowing that people value different things than others also adds to the intricate web of life. There are some that value people more than anything, while some put a super high focus on freedom or their well-being. Some also are all about the cash and things, and some also can think global or even for out of the atmosphere of this planet too! It is okay to want things, though the delicate balance is how to achieve what we wish for ethically, and with the incorporation of our respect for others, the universe, and life we meld together as a whole.

The shift of marketing ourselves is a tricky one too. I wanted to enlist the help of many of the people of Earth to bring Natalie to me (even if it's only a one-time meeting) and it's something that I don't want to manipulate. It is a fine line between me sharing my story, and finding people who want to help me, compared to making my objectives and using people to allow the dreams to unfold. I set a date of Christmas Day 2017 as the day to meet Natalie, and it led to severe cosmic disturbance. It's not something I comprehend as rational. I shall work for others and may benefit too by tilling seeds and helping us achieve our wants. I also know to enjoy the process of developing our story.

Even if I don't meet Natalie, I'm okay with that too. The things that I want are to abide by are my prerogatives, and also to ensure that I don't have to rely on others to unwillingly support me. I also wish for more than enough for myself so that I can share.

The 'clouds' that Gary spoke of (with D-Rock!) for me is that I want us each to have what we want. I want us each to find our Freedom Solutions resource-wise, and then add the additional layer that we're each to be happy and glad. I want to be able to benefit others by achieving our dreams, and that our wins will help others win also. A layer from Jennifer McLean is that when our wants are good for ourselves, that they too should be good for others, and also good for the world.

We need to know what our values are, and my hope is others will form their lives with integrity, kindness, and positive reciprocation.

There is a picture I found of four circles that I took from the Internet. I think it's an excellent key for people to know regarding themselves and their purpose(s) on planet Earth. I include the picture in this book, and as I wrote this, I thought of our story and the journeys that we're on. Everyone needs to know and find their paths, goals, wants; perhaps the picture may guide you as good seed.

Even though I had the idea to meet Natalie, I think that there's far much more to say about life and our world(s) than just my own story and desires. I want this book to convey something that will help others. The second circle is that the world needs.

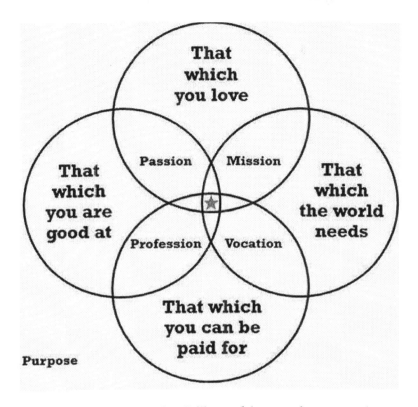

I talk of many things that I like and love and want, and even though I should not be over-confident, I believe that we need to be good at sharing life to help others.

This journey is not solitary. Even if I am alone at home or SCUBA diving in the coffee shop, my life is not just me. I think to include parts of other's lives into this; not just the advice I may have for others, not just the want to learn how to be a friend, though also the process of our journeys here in our shared life.

This planet is Earth, and worth is far more than cash and

things. This world is made up of many entities and not just us humans! We are not alone, and *I* am only one node in The Contialis.

In *The Fountains of Yesterday,* I want to share more of me, my story, and my messed up inner world. I want to help gather our today's and yesterdays into what we may gather for our futures. Natalie, you are one I'd like to meet, and even if our lives may not ever merge in a real-world meeting, you have guided me well. I shall return to the Earth much that I have learned from knowing you like another kind, and as a dear human being on this planet, you hold my soul.

You reminded me of my love, and I know of myself that my love may not be just for one specific person as I thought it had to be. When I find my lovestone, I will keep her well and tend to her. I also hope that that one gal that will be my lovestone will also stay entirely loyal… towards the point of forever, even if we're not there yet.

BUILD WITH SOMEONE

There is a whole premise and pull for what I do; I want to build *with* people. Sefrina and Josh (bro's before hoe's trumped by 'ladies first') chipped in $20 for a copy of *Finding Natalie*! I had copies of the book from a dear and cool gift from Ali. Ali gave me $100 to order twenty copies of the first book. He let me keep five copies and chipped in an extra twenty dollars: the five copies I received meant one for Josh and Sefrina, a copy for The Gale's as a wedding gift, a real copy for the Bradford's, and one copy for the Jennifer who was in chat with me the second morning after the release. It also meant a copy for Bill.

Jennifer shared her time and heart with me in the morning just after the release of book one. She also offered to buy a copy! I am glad for this. We went for a walk along Hope Slough, and I remember telling her how I want to earn enough money with my creative works to be self-sufficient. I also recall her telling me about her challenge of her inner mind, and it reminds me of a lot of negative things that people have said to me about my dreams and wants.

I've received lots of advice from some people that *is* good and right in my heart though. Like the comment of how it doesn't matter how many bones I throw if the dog wants a stick. The advice of how people may distance or not have an interest in my works if I use code or other languages. The opinion that I should perform my work for my wants and not just pander to people to earn a sale. There also is the lesson that I should learn and be clear about my intents and *why* I am doing things. Lastly, from the title of this chapter, to not do it all on my own.

The writing field is quite solitary. I heard from another about their concerns of how if no one reads or listens to what we've made, it can be discouraging. It's true. I have found myself asking "why do I even do this if no one is going to read?" Bring it back to the pinnacle Jet and how Gary said: "one is better than zero."

We do not do this all on our own!

My stories have carried me through time and space by having me as one with a lot of time on my own. I recall my Mom's statement of "it's a cast of thousands" and carry that into this book too. Many people are all integrated and aloof and intimidating themselves into our lives to push themselves into our story. Do not be used! Do not be fooled!

I know I do use a lot of manipulation and control tactics, though I note too that I also make my share of assumptions. There are a few key people that I had as 'car friends.' As of June of 2016, my car was off the road. Of the people I used to drive around, I've lost connection and frequent communication with almost all of them. I had a Facebook message from one of them that said: "so wish you had your car on the road still." My response "Me too. 2k albums sold would allow it." They followed with "just need to find a ride to Gilford Mall and back." The message cued me to think that the friend only cared that I had a car because of their need.

Some people say that those without money are in that

situation from a scarcity mentality. I don't believe that's always the case. It *is* true that some people have a lot less income than others and *have* to focus on their lack in the process of finding their Freedom Solutions. It's true that some people are in poverty, though, I don't think it's always from them focusing on that.

Back to the car friend situation. In January 2016, I almost needed to sell my car. One friend, who I drove around a lot, said they didn't think it was a good idea. My Dad conveyed something about "Oh, I wonder why not?" on the level of how that friend relied on me for transportation. My Dad thought it evident that they didn't want me to lose the car because it would affect them. This friend also is the only friend the messaged out me when I was in Italy in July 2016 to ask me how my trip was.

I've lost a lot of contact with friends because I can't meet their needs or help due to a lack of money. My Dad doesn't support the Natalie dream, and he also doesn't want me spending money on books to sell as he sees it as a frivolous waste. I see it as me striving to find a creative income.

I'm not going out into the world to find Natalie. I know that the real Natalie is one that has thousands of fans that want to meet her, and I don't think she should waste any of her time to find me either. It also doesn't diminish the fact that I have years and years of thoughts, energies, and delusions that I want to clarify as real or not.

I don't know if the energy that I've felt as Natalie is even real, let alone the famous one. I want to know what the truth is, though, and I work with life in line with my heart and desires.

I form an experience that I love to live. I want to do something substantial, even to the level of calling it epic, with my life. When I started the first book in 2013, the intended audience of that one book was one person. Even to the point of when I released *Finding Natalie*, the intent was to gather the world to encourage her to form a meeting with me. The morning after the release, I had a talk with Chandra that removed the curse and veil of the Natalie dream from my heart, spirit, and soul, and my mind and body felt free again. Natalie's shackles returned, though.

My intents and wants clarified in the three to five weeks since I put the first book on the internet. I'm *not* going to go searching or messaging for Natalie on the internet, though I am going to speak my heart. I want to meet Natalie, though she is no longer my primary objective in life.

I've also gained clarity about my music, my flowetics, and my recordings. I know I'm not a musician, I'm not an MC, nor am I a rapper. I shall, though, fortify and develop and cultivate my ability to write and speak rhymes. I'm *not* going to adjust my presentation and lyrics to lure people into buying my music, and I *am* going to learn ways to string words together; streams of rhymes can make sense, though why would people want to buy them?

I finish this book, and other publications, for the fact that *I* want to share my thoughts, ideas, and values with some. The use of correct English and structure is vital if I want my point to be understood, though my creative works are a massive part of this process, even if no one else cares.

(The key thing, though: some people care!)

FRAGMENTS OF INTENT

A conversation with a primary person reminded me of some key life things. We've been told to be ourselves. If I'm not creating for mass appeal, and I don't want to be something that is *not* myself, I must carry the same personal integrity and ethics into what I do with my creative works.

The sacrifices I make for staying true to myself cross over into and from these works. If I'm to create for money, people seem to be telling me that I need to make sense and conform to what's the norm. Some say to write about what people expect or to write like other people. I don't like that, and I won't. If told "it's better to be loved for who we are than loved for something we're not," and I agree. I do want to be loved for who I am, and not for what I want people to believe.

I know I may not make big money at this point, and that's okay, I may not need it. My pushing of the first book to my friends, and also the promotion of my music, comes from my desire for an income. I want to be self-sufficient, and I don't need millions of dollars to do it. If I break down the numbers and talk of my Freedom Solution, I only need ten or fifteen thousand units of 'Me' sold each year. My goal is 6,000 units per month.

"But Rob!? I thought you said you don't want to create things to earn money!" I also told you I don't want to rely on the government or my family for money. How else shall I make money if I can't force myself to work a job that I'll hate or schitz out at and either get fired or have to quit?

The planet we live on requires most people to have an income. I know my ideal income is $5,000 per month;

$60,000 a year. If I make about $2 from an album or book, I divide $60k by $2 to find that 30k units need be sold a year to people that care, or are interested, in what I do to support myself. Your FS (Freedom Solution) number is probably different, though I was given the advice too to know what we need, what we want, and think about how to achieve that.

That rewinds to the title of this chapter, Build *With* Someone. I choose to build with those that will reciprocate and know that I cannot tend to everyone. If I am to create and form my life with people, then I best be a part of their lives and reality too.

There have been times in my life where I thought (from my Mom's cast of thousands statement) that all sorts of people were in a Natalie conspiracy. I believed that people were playing their roles in my life to form a chance for her and me to meet. I now no longer care if that's the case, and will tell you all why.

If Natalie was, or even still is, pulling all the strings, I'm tired of being played like a marionette or puppet. I had been too focused on her and doing the 'right things' for *her* which blends in Kevin's advice, that I should do it for *me*. People have told me: "Be selfish until you can be generous." I want to help other people, and shall, though I also must find a way to support myself, and know I can't do it on my own.

My Mom has wanted me to have a plan for my life. I haven't always had that. I can't tell my Mom what the idea is because she doesn't like it. A friend had made a comment that got me thinking. They said my Dad doesn't love me unconditionally if he thinks I shouldn't spend money on books. I know that

FRAGMENTS OF INTENT

my Dad does have unconditional love for me, though heard in refute that he doesn't have that if he told me not to spend money on books to share and sell.

Right now, when I wrote this, money wise, I was poor. I have to rely on the government's PWD and some additional support for the majority of my income. Chip-ins from a few people for buying books are not yet anywhere near what I need to support myself. Someone buying my book at this point is a showing of love and care and support of me, my work, and my dreams.

My Mom thinks my first book is inconsequential and I'm so dearly amazed and glad of the very few people that have bought a copy up to now. Also, since I don't consider myself a musician, I am wavering on the idea of myself selling albums. I want to work and write for people and counsel them to find their dreams and then help achieve them. I hold a lot of value for some, and though I'm terrible at the business, marketing, and push promotion required for some of what I do, I also note that I carry knowledge, and heart, enough to help others on *their* paths too.

Please allow me enough to support myself so that I can help others achieve and receive that they want too. Please let me earn enough trust and respect in myself for and from others so that we all can work together to form and achieve our dreams. Please allow all people to find themselves, their Freedom Solutions, and the ability to live, love, and thrive and learn, create, play and pray. I'd like for us all to have enough to share with other people and not lack.

Please let me work on this planet for Global, Individualistic, and Collective PLUR for the benefit and protection of life. Let a divine will of life help heal, support, nurture, and construct an ability for people to be glad for, and cherish, the lives of others, as well as their own. Amen.

You've not read this yet, though the paths crossed. I work for God on this planet, even if I cannot run around preaching the will of His Son.

DARE TO DREAM

You're a friend that I didn't initially trust. Your statements of "it's not an issue unless you make it an issue" have spun back on me, and I shall make atonement. I also twist what you said into a different saying of *"If you want to be the solution, you shall be."* In this book, I've not described what extended PLUR is, though I know we'll have a full conversation about it.

The credo of PLUR (Peace, Love, Unity, and Respect) holds in my heart and soul, though we know my mind gets in the way far too often. Being riddled with fear, paranoia, and insecurities are part of the cross that I bare, and though we see the facts from different viewpoints, I've not entirely honoured your fearlessness, care, and devotion. The advice I received was to "trust no one," and it spins in with a different value or idea. There's a polar shift of a viewpoint; that fear or a lack of trust shows as opposites of love, sometimes.

If I want to be a friend, then I must learn to trust. I have a fear of being vulnerable, yet am okay to talk. I must share my information and ideas with people, though my heart still holds my mind to the point of neurosis. It's a fear which limits me from being a real true friend to some in a few ways. You are so much more confident and bold, yet I've also been told not to compare.

After a week in early October 2016, I held much in my mind. I seemed to have had paralyzed myself with fear, doubt, and

73

an inability to trust. I'd been finding my deep flaws and intents, yet still, I need to cleanse some ideas to perform the correct and right actions. I've been so focused on my own 'stuff' that I've not been able to be a proper friend or support for others. I change and evolve, yet didn't step up for you at one crucial point when you needed me. It makes me feel sad.

You too would say to learn from my mistakes. I do. You also would tell me not to be something or someone that I'm not. I won't. The facts of my fears limiting me so strongly is not something I like, as it's not a win or benefit for anyone in full regard. I admire how brave and real you are, and I'm sorry for not being as courageous or kind or 'there' as I could have been. I also am kindly reminded that you care and support your friends with devotion. Thank you, Gideon.

I wish not to shower with praise, and I also want to speak the truth. I want to let you know about a whole bunch of other people from my past, and tell you my stories about how I've become who I am. I don't know *your* history, I've barely asked. I've not contacted very often, and I also think people don't want explanations. The times where I've said I've failed as a friend clearly show my lack of care and confidence in some many ways. Rewind to earlier though Rob, if you want to be the solution, you shall be!

I want to talk to them again soon. I won't message right now, though, because I forget not about the plan and the plot — the dualism of me being full of wishing for care and support limits with behaviours of fear and paranoia. Know of the polar idea of there being a line between truth and trust or love, and by me not trusting you enough, I've perchance teetered the boundaries of how I am a true friend.

FRAGMENTS OF INTENT

I called upon another friend today. It seems that there are issues between other people in both friendship and communal layers with me. My want is that we all work together and communicate our mistakes or errors and grievances so that we can all be okay with each other. I'll support a few people, and I know I often have lacked understanding that. I seem to miss other people's points when they explicitly share them with me, and I'm not fond of the amount of patience and forgiveness sometimes required from those that are a friend; and even those that aren't.

This section also should not be used as an explanation or defence. It's part of my process and a way to communicate when I'm unable to do so in other ways. I want to know it will reach you through sight, and not just the mind as it formed. I wish you'd talk on the phone with me more and that you'd ask more questions. I'll give you answers, and to twist in, *not* with the form of removal!

Since I've also said 'all the intellect and deceit' before, the lack of knowing what true intents are also guided my choices to be wary and cautious. For what has happened, I can't change it. For what is now, I still don't fully know. For what I'll do today, I'll keep at my work, seed my wishes, and know we are part of the solution, even if I'm often afraid to be an active part.

I honour you, you have me as a friend, and I also request we can talk about concerns about our situations. Though we've not spoken on the phone recently, I hope you may forgive me and my fear. I also hope we can discuss my lack of being there as a friend when you truly needed it. I'm glad you have friends that are honest and genuine support. You are so

75

much more courageous and set, stable, and bold than I am.

As much as a weak thing to say, I am such a fragile, delicate, and tentative human being. I'm glad you don't live with many of the same fears and insecurities that I possess. My mental health is so often near or clear to be an issue that I'm wondering how I'll ever be stable enough to live. The previous chapter talked of building with people, and I am coping. I'll be okay, I know.

I lacked insight and intuition into your situation that one morning you called. By the fact that you were smoking a cigarette, I should have known something severe had happened as you had previously quit. I still don't know what caused you your issue (what the problems are or were) and that had me feeling a bit confused. We also remember how I don't want to display sadness or be a downer. I should have understood that you were at your Mom's as a refuge and it was a sign that something was entirely wrong.

The shift from the past to the future. The idea now not 'what happened' to instead 'what will happen.' Mirrodin sir! We shall endure! Shift into a different shared idea or question. What is my intent? What will I do? I'll keep at my work and note that my work is of that I shared earlier in the book. I also shall be a friend. I don't know how my muddle clears, yet I still want to talk.

I remind myself I do care a lot for some people. So often I find myself being a waffle, and though I care a lot sometimes, it's after the point of being needed. I've neglected to step up, and also give my intents as one to talk with people about issues to help resolve them. We develop with ourselves, with

FRAGMENTS OF INTENT

each other, and the work of being a friend is not one that I'm so great at tending.

The fact I'm so wishy-washy, and not action based, has probably skewed some others from being my friend too. I have a want and intent of helping people with their lives, though I also must recall to not focus so much on the mistakes I've made. You remind me that my heart's care and devotion, and even though sometimes latent, is strengthening significantly.

What I can let you know in this chapter is not just what I have typed up to now, or what we shall talk about today. I add this as absolute fact and caution; you are one of the most important people that I have in my life. I pray well that if I place my full trust in you and God that my wishes may become solid and devoted pillars for much more than a few.

The next wishes that I have are different and varied. I hope that you're fully honoured and rewarded as having a pure soul and heart too. You cue me up to the Glass House and remind me that you've deeply affected me and the course of my life. Even the seeded Natalie posted in my awareness pointed to me writing this chapter. I could barely think of today, though I pray and wish and hope that your life also may be seeded with more love than we can yet comprehend. Another wish and prayer are that the only Martyrs we ever know in real life are those in Soul Sisters or Spectrasoul Modern decks.

Religiously, I still don't know how the death of Jesus could save another. I'm far too young in my spiritual understanding, yet I also wish we need not rely on false hope.

I shall not preach to you, though thank you for visiting me.

And after your visit, though, back to the plough. We shall build!

The future and the world that we live in has yet to unfold. You may be back here again, so I'll keep parts of this book open for the future too. The work of building our future and getting our goals and dreams on paper is something that I recorded. I don't yet understand the plan of how to get to the Glass House, though I do know how it functions and how it forms.

The idea of the home is similar to how I want my current place to be; just it's a far more expansive project and design. I'll tell you of the plan at the first meeting we form for the focus sessions. I'm dearly glad that you visited, and though I've been so fearful and uncertain, there is value in that too.

We've kept me more humble and grounded than I would be otherwise. I also hope to be bold and kind to you in the future. I thank you so exceptionally much for being a friend. Though I've made so many mistakes and errors, I remind myself to have hope. Vision and resolve work for many more than a few, including you.

The reminder that value is not always money is a point I've sometimes neglected. I'm glad you get that and know it's understood. I also like and love how you know that people working together for each other is not just a want or a wish, yet instead what we set our intents to do and shall continue to do. I have a layer of fear about my future, and faith in God and the process allows our friends and family to help assist our lives too. Grazie sempre!

FRAGMENTS OF INTENT

From the title of this chapter, I shall allow myself to reveal what my dreams are. We shall dare to dream! You know Natalie is out there, and even if I can't go seeking her out, the Glass House is also to form. I neglected to mention how extended PLUR is part of that plan. My dream, for now, is to earn, cultivate, and develop so that I'm allowed the privilege and blessing to be able to help build other people's homes and lives.

The reminder about meeting to talk about our futures is a crucial seed you gave me. There is a defining node in this; we work together, and for, each other to guild lives we'll love to assist.

My role and function for the next while are to keep the contialitic works evolving. We assure my home is a safe and welcome place for people to gather and joke a bit with you that the Magic *is* the gathering. I have lots to do for myself too; this book is part of my healing process. I'm glad you assist, and though you left my place a while ago, I hope we gather again in the future.

I thank you explicitly for the seeds you have sown and have shared too. I may be getting a bit repetitive or over-focused on this, so perchance a time point to shift between the books. I'm in the forming of *Shared Node (Key to Me)* too, and your link to asking of *Finding Natalie* holds you now in all three. Words are not adequate to share the appreciation I have for you!

We shall speak again!

ROBERT KOYICH

TAKE A BREATH

(This is going to be an epically long journey. I need Your help!)

A prayer and a wish are that you may use these books as your own. Since some don't yet have a belief in God, I'll address some to the universe and use the word 'You.' It's also as a prayer and wishes for others because prayer lets us focus.

I thank You for a layer of protection, truth, light, and love. I also ask for humility and strength to surround us and keep us safe. Please allow us to thrive. To not just exist, though to thrive!

I thank You for allowing me what I have and for giving me the seeds to life. Even if I'm held in despair and degradation at times, I'm sorry for not trusting enough in You, my friends, my family, and others on this planet.

I thank You for the codes and the ideas you've allowed me to be aware of, and even if they are not all from Your source, I thank You for creating and teaching me.

I ask that my abilities, knowledge, presence, and life may be extended and used as a way to benefit people on this planet. I wish not to be so self-focused and that I don't have to incite or instill additional issues. What I ask is I may be a vassal for many more than a few, including You.

I thank You for the awareness that you've allowed me, and for letting me grow, evolve, and develop. I also ask that You may be an excellent and loving guide for all. Thank You too for my work and books.

Please let people be good, kind, and faithful. Please allow us safety so we may tend to the works, likes, goals, hopes, and dreams of many. Please let me be humble and meek, and also that I'm not manipulated, used, or abused.

I thank You for letting me learn about myself, and I ask that I may learn, understand, and hear from others also. Please allow us to plant the seeds, tend the fields, and find abundance in our gardens.

Please let me learn and keep the ability to set myself aside for other people when they need support. Let people not need to be protected, and let PLUR be a guiding motive and action.

Thank You for insight, hope, goals, and appreciation. Let us cultivate, develop, and earn the right to live and love, and let me speak and write the truth. Let me be compassionate and empathetic, and please allow the trust that I give to people to hold in full honour. Do not let us get twisted with negativity.

Balance our situations and restore them to and with extended and global PLUR. Let the lovestones and shoulsmen work together, guild, and build with each other, and I thank You also for reminding me of the commitments that I've made; to You, to myself, to others, and the world of Earth.

I am only one person on this planet, and though I may not yet know what the future holds, let me build homes for others and myself so that we can tend to the lives of Earth. Let our prospects entwine with goodness, truth, love, and joy.

FRAGMENTS OF INTENT

Please let our faith, hope, and effort be fueled by positive growth, discovery, and understanding, and allow others also to have and share. I thank You for the facts You've given me to work with and share, and even if there's such a vast network and knowledge base that I have no idea about, let me, please, be granted the ability to live and thrive as I have been allowed to up to even now... Amen.

I had gone to bed near 10 PM the night before to sleep, get up, and walk to Chilliwack Victory church. I couldn't get to sleep until after midnight and did not wake up on time to walk to Victory. I had almost submitted to missing church again, though saw a public post from the Pastor on Facebook that had conveyed or said: "Go to church, even if not Victory today." I chose to go, and for that I'm glad.

I heard Ian Green speak at First Avenue Christian Assembly that day, both in the AM service and at a far smaller gathering in the afternoon. I learned and became aware of some things that helped seed my intents as to how to help. I'm still very young in my journey of life, and though I also know that I'm one who believes in having the universe and peace of the Kingdom of God rule here on Earth, I also don't want to abuse or scare people away from being apart.

I have been Earthly in my journey, and the wish and sharing is part of my work here on this planet. Sometimes I may be a bit disruptive, though it is for a good cause. From Ian Green's talk, he reminded me that if I'm to work for the Kingdom of God, that I also have a blessing of knowing so many people are not convicted of being a part of it yet. I must tend to some as saplings and seeds and remember it is a delicate and fragile balance. I am not God, though I work for

83

Him and His son and believe my music is used well by them and the Spirit.

Because I'm very young in my Christian faith, I still have a lack of understanding about how the world works. I learn how I help expand and keep watch for those that don't believe, and this is where my writing becomes a tool and part for Kingdom work. I have a concern I'll push people away by talking about spiritual things, though I also have the want that others be kept and held dear in their own lives. I prosper and pay homage to God, though I have a fear of becoming too preachy.

My thoughts, ideas, beliefs, and attitudes have shifted a lot over the past two weeks. The point of nearly getting beaten up, a night where God told me of his anger towards me, and intense pain in my back is a strong spiritual, physical, and psychic guidance. My own mental and spiritual attitudes are genuine to me. I have been more tentative regarding some of what I think and do, and believe that my ideas and what I write are a substantial part of the process. I will develop and use them for good.

There is a luxury of having the ability and tools to write, record, and share. Writing is a responsibility and one thing that I'm glad for having. I love sharing my ideas and thoughts, though there also is a balance of what I do, how I do it, and how and why (and for and to who) I relay what I form.

Finding Natalie was a very self-focused book. I was honed in on a dream that had caught my heart many years ago, and I had become obsessed with Nat. I don't know what value my books have for the world if it's 'all about me,' and I'm still learning to be other minded or focused. I remind myself that my obsessions can lead to good work, and know this too with the Word and work of God.

Some people have no interest or awareness of or about God. Talking about spirituality is a very dangerous topic for many people, and personal revelation and acceptance is something that comes through time. It may be very different for each, though I have a lack of understanding of Jesus. I'm more attuned to some spiritual things now, though I also don't want to twist the ideas or premises of other's beliefs. I shall not use the church for my gain.

When first writing this part of the book, I went back and looked at the four circles picture. When I started writing this Fountain, I was very bottom circle focused. I also seemed to think that what I liked and loved are writing and recording and that I'm good at them too. I was pushing and focused on earning an income with my skills, though also thought that what I made wasn't part of what the world needs. I now seem to think I have a lot of ideas and guidance that the world may need or use *and* don't feel right about pushing my mission only to form an income.

I find the teetering balance. I think of learning and teaching while remembering some don't like to be told. There needs to be, I think, a desire to learn and take in information. I have that desire sometimes while I may not always seem to learn. In the world, there is a lot of need for things, including learning, so I heed that. I may have been more focused on surface issues before.

I want to put myself towards helping with transformation and not only social justice and action. With some of my conversations, I've been limiting myself by not talking about spiritual things with people because a lot of the people I know aren't believers. The ideas from Ian Green remind me of how we can and should work for other people with this process too.

Another Magic player at a card shop held an idea. The premise is to find the causes of issues and dealing with those sources of thought or behaviour. If we can see the reason of action, we can adjust so that the problems don't occur. The player was talking from a criminology viewpoint, yet this also makes sense with social work and also relationship issues, even if not a part of this chapter or book.

We know there are lots of issues in our society like the local homelessness issues or global food, water, shelter, and sanitation issues. There also is the advice not to get too big or out there for some things. Some people have said to 'start at home.' What Ian was talking about was how, for homelessness, that even if people are given homes to live in, there need to be additional skills, programs, and supports. People need to be able to not only live, though maintain those lives. I have often found myself knowing that we can't just throw money at problems.

We need to bring some people back into society. I'm on the outer edges of some parts of life regarding being a contributing member of the community. I am without a job and relying on support, and even if I do find a job, I can only handle part-time work. With the state of my creative works at the point of writing, the books didn't seem a viable path.

With the first book so Natalie and Rob-centric, I didn't think it would help much with other people's lives.

I have other books in process at this point, though this book is for sharing our process. I have a concern that some who aren't Christian based may sway from reading this, and I may hold back on the spiritual quotient for other books. A link to *Built from Within* is a different book to write and read as a social seed.

The reason this chapter is titled *Breath In, Breathe Out* was because I had almost quit smoking. I had formed a prayer with the wish, intent, and clarity I found after committing to stop. It's apparent that I didn't, though I'm also more aware of some mental and spiritual things from smoking.

I've been a smoker since 1994-1995. It's been a central part of who I am, and like my attitude with some jobs, I don't like how I've defined or have been defined by it. I sometimes love smoking, yet also don't want to be a smoker. I've used tobacco as a coping mechanism for so long, and I've been using the addiction as a crutch. I have been going through issues in my life and heard that the stress of quitting might be too much right now.

The differences in resource or status based social disparity are something that I'm aware of too. As a smoker, I have, at points, held worth or value in myself as being one to help with tobacco. There is a blend in this. I want people's wants and needs provided, yet I also don't want to hold power over others. I have a concern about how some could be angry at me for having access to resources while some others don't.

I found myself talking about how I wish people could all be

on the same level. I don't want people to all be the same, yet I hope that we'll learn to work together for all. The layers of authority and difference in access to resources concern me, yet maybe that's because I'm an idealist. I hold a desire for a utopian society where all people can have what they need and want. It's rad when people can do what they want without crossing other people's boundaries.

The notion that each of us has different needs is valid, though we also hopefully learn to tend the needs of different people. I hope we can care for individual people and animal's collective beings in the world in which we live. What the world needs is what I hope to tend to, though remember many people on Earth have different individual and collective needs too.

Once we can cover and acquire the basic needs of each person (Maslow's Hierarchy), we can help work forward and beyond. The thing that concerns me is some people don't yet have their food, water, and shelter. I am an exceptionally fortunate person, though I cannot tend to the needs of many if I'm only one at this point.

So, breathe in and breathe out. Clear your mind, your heart, and your spirit. We share the world of Earth, and we need to remember that we're all on the same planet. I want to work with and for people, and I definitely shall. I also need to learn how to give, earn, and share *a lot* of love, light, luck, and life!

It's a *shared* journey.

DRAW THE MANA

You've supported me so very well through the years. There are times in the past I used to get angry at you, and it stems back to when you and Mom had divorced. I recall us talking about this a few years ago and how you said: "It's been 20 years!" It's true, and many other things guild like the towns we saw in Italy in 2016.

I sometimes like to use metaphors and ideas that are not understood by others. We remind me to use language that others know and understand, even if my obsessive regularity of random is something unique. It *is* a part of me. You've shown and demonstrated unconditional love for me, and though you don't have full faith or belief in me and my dreams, I still thank you for also keeping me more rational than I could be.

The idea of the Glass House surfaces again, and part of that want, dream, vision, and goal is so that I can live close to you and Sarah. Mom has said that she likes how I'm optimistic, though the layers also know that I can be foolish. Right now, I don't even know how to support myself, let alone have a family or find income enough to build the home. Your comments about my music being successful only if I'm 'really really lucky' also twinges me. I know from the current day situation that I'm *not* making money with my music, and that too is why I adjusted the channels I'm using.

I'd like us to talk in person again. The fact that you and I usually only get to see each other once every two years is not so fantastic, though a lot better than not at all. I wonder about your views of me and what growth you've seen in my attitude and behaviours between when we meet. Christmas 2015 and January 2018 were two points where we visited in Australia and interacted together.

I don't want to set the music and writing dreams aside. There is still the Natalie issue, and right now I note it may be a problem and not an idea to hold as a goal. The fact that I've gone so many years with her as a post stuck in my mind has not gone on so well for me. When I released the first book, I went through some severe feelings, emotions, and stress, and if Natalie is love, then should she not bring me joy and gladness and not fear and despair? I mentioned earlier that you told me to not even think about her, and I try to do that.

Another layer is how you're not a Christian believer. I wonder about your roles on Earth beyond just being my father; you're a friend to quite a few people around the world, and I admire and love your attitude and abilities. Even if you give guidance to me with a subtle force, and not a direct command, I like much of what you've taught me. It wasn't so comfortable with having you away for so long, and though I was furious at you and Sarah when you and Mom first broke up, I accept our situations now. I also commend you for moving back in grade eight to try and work it out again, even if it didn't.

Our most recent visit was a wonderful one. The visit reminded me, though, I still carry a lot of my own emotional and spiritual baggage. There was one dinner in Italy where I got despondent that was cued by a Natalie post on Instagram.

When I saw her post and found she was not in Italy when we were at that time, I twisted myself inwards into sadness and irritability. Other's shouldn't have to suffer for my emotional damage and despair.

When we were in Orvieto, there was a strong Natalie intuition and thought focus too. It might have been that I'd been reading an early version of the first book, though it was like that if I played my cards right that Natalie would magically show up. My delusions have told me she knows me, and there have been many times I've anticipated meeting her. I don't want to play games; I want to build and work for life and lives.

On a trip to the Sydney apartment a few years ago, I was cleaning dishes after a meal one night. At that moment I knew I didn't *need* Natalie to complete my life; that I'm whole and complete on my own. This moment was a crucial point for me because when I was in the psych ward, I was so overly focused on the idea of her and I that I thought I'd never have been able to live without her.

Where am I now with the Natalie topic? I know that she is too much of a focus sometimes for myself to think about for my health. I wonder of therapeutic ways and ideas to cleanse the stain in my soul from obsessing about her so much, and I carry on with my life and work. Talking about her and my thoughts need to be processed to clean my innards. I'm a very stained and fractured soul, though working and talking with other people, or writing sometimes, is a way for me to heal, process, and purge.

I'm sorry, Dad, for having so many messed up and anxious

thoughts and also for being so focused on what I want. What I'd like, instead, is to build a life where I'll be okay and thrive without relying on you or the government for support. You know I believe in God, and I also note that you are my father that I prefer to call Dad. Both you *and* God have helped me so much through the years. Though I sometimes don't understand how you are so much of my life, I've gotten muddled with the religious ideas too.

I thank you so much, Dad, for being a crucial and critical influence, support, and guide in my life. Some friends don't like or know their own Dad. I'm so exceptionally fortunate to know you and to be able to see you, even if so rarely. One thing that Mom wants me to gather is to form a plan for my life. You and her both know that I'll keep making things and working on friendships and other relationships, though the actual question of 'How will you make your money Robert?' is not one that I yet know.

I've plowed the fields and created so many seeds of work, yet haven't yet been able to succeed in finding myself and my books again used for a purpose or value for another. That's why I write. I have a lot of information to share, I have some ideas and encouragement for others, and I also remember that even if I have proper intent, that it takes many more than a few to help me and let me assist others in their lives.

My books are very selfish right now. The Fountain, *Searching for Tomorrow*, started with the idea to be life support for others, and just like *Finding Natalie*, it's turned to me writing randomly outwards to a few people that matter. I don't see how this can be a commercial release that will bring value to another. My intents may not be in the correct or proper

FRAGMENTS OF INTENT

place as my wants may still be too much be a focus. Instead of forming works that will benefit other readers, it's kind of like that I'm just a persistent novelty act.

And yet I continue…

When I was writing this chapter, you were in Cambodia. Cambodia links to some of my dreams with Survivor. If I ever get the chance to compete on that show, you're the one family member that I'd love to meet there also to compete. Mom has been incredible support, though the layer of working *with* you is something I desire. When we formed the communication cupboard in your garage, it was a pretty cool thing. I love working with you, and note I carry a bit of sadness that we didn't live in the same country when I was growing up during junior high and high school. We also know that Mom did do a pretty good job as a single mother.

I wrote a bit about you in my first book. There was a lot of text that focused on dream girl, and since you don't support that dream, I note, maybe, like Mom, the book may not be an easy one for you to read. I also wonder about your viewpoint on a few other people that have affected me a lot in my journey, though have neglected to ask or mention.

I like and love the idea of business and entrepreneurship. That's why I wanted to buy and sell Magic cards; I like the idea of profit and sales. We also know that with my creative work, that it's not quite filling the 'need' circle in the four circles picture. I know I'm not confident that I can help others with their issues when I seem not to have found my solutions yet. How can I gain knowledge, skills, credibility and trust to help others if I've not demonstrated that for myself?

I also want to say thank you for the gifts you gave to me when I was in the hospital. I remember you and Mom bringing me Taco Bell when I was in Grey Nuns, and I remember how Norma would visit and help buy me cigarettes when I was in the ward. You also gave me a computer when in the UBC hospital that I could use for recording when there.

I think of Gary again with this. He has explicitly shared how his family, like his Dad, are the most primary and essential part of his life. Gary is one that I look up to a lot as he has shown success and development, and also has taught me some of my moral lessons. The values of trust and integrity are qualities that I want to develop further in myself, and even you might remind me to do some things for myself, and not just for others. I get myself sorted out and stable so that I also can also assist others from and with a firm and solid foundation.

I love visiting you and Sarah. I thank you both so very dearly, kindly, and explicitly for being patient, kind, and extremely forgiving through the years. You let me come to be who I am now. I know that I have very much been living freely and that many people may not understand how and why I'm allowed to live. I also note that the value of meritocracy and *earning* my place in life *is* also what I value and tend. You and Sarah worked so diligently and effectively to secure the spot where you are now, and that inspires and motivates me to make my life too!

I turn inwards to my awareness. Our relationship as father

FRAGMENTS OF INTENT

and son has so often been all about me. I have been needy and so self-focused sometimes when I want to know a lot more about you too. Technology is a precious and crucial thing for us to keep in contact, and I thank you for giving me the time, space, and grace to grow as a person. I haven't forgotten about the book I gave you for Christmas and hope that you'll complete the writing in the different sections of the book. I want to learn more about you too.

I find the twist between the mad, sad, and glad triangle. I feel sad that others don't have Dads that they like or love, and there is a twist of how I'm afraid of another being mad at me because I'm glad about my Dad. I don't like how some others are sad, and that twists me up and finds me harmonizing with the emotion sometimes. My friends have commented that they think that I'm sad sometimes, even when I don't feel it. I've had issues with being angry in the past, though I'd prefer to be balanced out, peaceful, and content compared to exquisite joy.

Another thing you know of me is that things sometimes change quickly and abruptly with me. When there is a long-running thread or issue that's been at me a lot that I think things need to be processed and resolved. My unemployment is a key one, and we also know I want to earn my income and not rely on you and the government. Another part of that is that I also don't want to only create for money. Like, when I make a recording, it's not made with the intent of income. A thing about my process is that I like to create, so I make things. I'd also like to seed purpose and fulfill a function. If it goes to the four circles, it's that that I want to do, things that I'm good at and love doing (the writing), and using them to fulfill a need so that I can earn money.

95

Some people know the business principle to think of finding the solutions to problems as a way to earn money. Maybe that's how I'm more a passion based person? I use my love for a function to perform a profession or vocation that includes my likes and loves. The thing about me being solo and author/artist and an awful entrepreneur is that I don't know how to present value, the solution. I am terrible at selling things. I provide information and ideas to fulfill a need for others, though a lot of what I've made hasn't had a lot of success.

My Earthly wants though (not money, the purpose part), is also something that I don't want to taint. I don't want to sacrifice my truths or be cash based in my intents. I have a layer of wanting to succeed with love and life and find my pathway to a prosperous and cohesive future. It's a muddle. The competing ideas and pulls of a few central ideas are in the mould of how I manage to stumble through the present to the future. Integrity and values help make sure I do the right things.

I must be cautious that I don't lure myself with things or people that could drag me down. I know with smoking that it's a primary part of my life, and I also have known that it's affecting me mentally and spiritually. When I was at the group home, smoking was a major social part of my life. We know that me having cigarettes, a car, or money in the past has had me used for having those things. That may be why I have so little money-wise; because I have a subconscious belief that I will be used or manipulated to dispense items or car rides if I have them.

I also love having my car on the road. I lost some car friends when I took my car off the street, and I'm now not able to get to and from places so quickly. I also have my home a place where I like to be sometimes. The 'sometimes' part is that I don't like isolation and want to have more visitors. Having no car also means, for now, not being able to interact with quite a few people because I can't get myself or them to or from our respective homes.

The Glass House though! That's an idea that I still want to happen. The idea for the home is to have it as a creative centre where people will be able to visit and use me for building their futures. We shall have people visit and spend a few days to a week to focus entirely on their work, relationships, projects, and businesses. I see the home as a place for people to gather and build. I, maybe, just haven't yet earned the right and blessing of having visitors that want to be here to talk about life. We shall gather though, I hope.

Anyhow, Dad, thank you for being love support and for guiding me and tending to me while letting me grow wild, free, and with a conscience. I hope to be a Dad one day too, and I hope that the home my family and I live in can be built close to you and Sarah. That's for a decade from now, so a lot of work to do between then and now, and that's okay.

ROBERT KOYICH

SOME QUESTIONS TO ASK

I want this chapter to be a gathering of questions that we should be answering: problems of and for ourselves, our friends, our family, and for this world; some we may not yet have answers for. I think, though, that we as people should be asking more questions of each other and ourselves. The thread of how these pages form and process may help us gather a more clarified perspective for ourselves. These books help an understanding of our place in this world.

How can we ensure we honour all lives? How can we help others with things and resources if we have none? How can we develop our dreams without getting called down for being too ambitious? Will people band together for, or against our world? How can we place trust in our wants, goals, and dreams if we can garner no support? How can I find myself amongst people that I can love and care for? Is it okay to want to care and support so many different people, even if I don't know them well?

Where are we going to be in our lives? Will we find our soulmates? Is dreaming a good thing for me, or am I just another wayward fool? Why can't I have the ability to heal people physically? Do I have the ability to do good and improve this world? If I am isolated so often, how can I tend the gardens of other people's lives? Do people even want me to help? Where should I bring myself forward to seed the fields and yields of tomorrow?

How does her hug feel? Is it that I'm too focused on 'being real'? How many layers are there that show that I want *real* love, and not just an imaginary deal? How can we let each of our beings heal?

Will my heart learn to love? Where and when shall we again lay down in a grassy field and see all the stars above? Shall there be time to share our heart, or will they merely want to cart me away into another day? How can I help them? Do they know I'm still learning how to be a human? Where can I take them on a trip to show them the fathoms of my being?

How clearly into the future can we each be shared if held in our soul? Am I even allowed to carry a partial role? What should I do if I cannot seem to have self-control? Where can I find the thread wind around the spool to remind my being that I do have some ideas that prove I'm *not* just a fool? Am I here? Why would they want me gone? How can I show other people that they've been playing me like a pawn?

Will they remember my father, Ron? Will Aeris seem to understand that the jewels of the land share my life years before we start to find out our waters in the sand?

Will love correctly stand? Will I yet even meet the first tender kiss, let alone the ring upon her hand? Will the world help us? Will the world help itself? Can I find the lucrative cutie wiggle her way up to the seat where we may place me up aside on the reef's shelf? Will I be able, even, to help my own belief?

Why haven't I been asking enough questions? Why haven't I been able to gather a gal? Why am I still so neurotic and twisted up in my own words that I've not yet seen that some

FRAGMENTS OF INTENT

are reaching out to me? If I'm a sapling, from a seed, then who planted this future tree? Will I be strong enough to stand up and rightly help them sip from the cup? Will I again be allowed to have a cat? Will I ever meet her pup?

Should I leave her alone? Should I tell others the things I don't condone? Will my mother's advice help pay the price for me being allowed to evade Heaven and Hell? Are we still allowed to live for many decades more in this Earthly planet and zone granted for us each to evolve as well?

When will I throw away the addiction? How can I find myself *not* to be a terrible affliction? Shall I slip past the point of poetic ruse and find ways for my heart to love and help others pay their dues? If I was one who had nothing, would I also act like those that I accuse of being ones to abuse, ruse, and use?

Can we please let the Ocean meet the Sea? Do they think I'm a weed and not a tree? Is it that some are yearning to hear me speak when I am sometimes too timid and meek? Can I please mix the A's and T's and C's and G's in the DNA's philosophies?

Have I done too much damage already? Is it that I am ready to meet her, and still must wait another few years? What happens when the smoke clears? Will she know me? Can I show that the lives we live earn in ways that others think are only free? How have I devoted myself to one I've never met when I can't even find myself to say or show I have a love for those not forgotten and forgiven yet?

May I help you? Would you like me just to listen or hear? Would you care for me to share a story? Would you like me to be there across from you and say not a single word? Would you want to be an angel, yet not have to die to fly free across the sky for every reason of why? Will you let me shed a tear? Will you let me cleanse my fear? Shall we find our own being enough, without needing anyone else to see, be near, or hear?

Can I please tell you what I mean? Like, will you give me the chance to speak, not to interrupt, and let me say to you how so dearly important you are to me? Even if you won't let me talk, can you please let me take a peek into your heart to find that grain of sand you left in it decades ago? Do you know how a pearl forms? Do you too think we hold in the same shell, yet still have no idea who each of us, and others, are?

Will you let me speak my shame? Will you let me repent my loss? Can you please tell me how Jesus dying upon the cross forgives my sins? Why do they believe me to be untrue? Why can't I share the signs and signals too? Will my heart learn to understand the depths of despair that I had put you through by not believing in you, True?

Can I please make amends? Can I let her know that what she wants is more than friends? Can our dear wondrous mind find a kind word to think or speak instead of calls that remind me not to be so meek? May I be so bold as to hold the dream? Does the horse assist in creating the team to share and keep the world in His palm? To know that sometimes the words and worlds of life need some time to calm?

Can I please stop for a moment? Can you please let me know who matters to you most? Can I please remind you also that I don't even know how or what we can be if I ever seem to

FRAGMENTS OF INTENT

understand what *is* between us?

Can I please set myself aside for a bit? Can I please slow down and regroup? Can I please ask the Dear Heavenly Father to remind us why we are held here in this linguistic soup?

I'm, sometimes, a sad, sombre soul. I'm one who's loved some that I think I should never have. I'm a child that is older than many adults, yet still hasn't had the faith, strength, or courage to grow up. Again, though, I'm glad.

I'm glad that we have a home to live in now. I'm happy that some have dreams and wondrous notions of crossing the different continents and oceans. I'm thankful that I sipped the potions or her smile, even if all the while I knew she wouldn't meet and give me the blessing of denial.

I'm glad to know my future cats. I may never let go of some things, and I had shackled myself to a tree of where we come from. I have called myself a sapling, and know not who's the one who loves me well enough to give me water and a pot in which to grow.

I am sometimes sad. I also sometimes am meek. I have, at points, been afraid to speak. I fear to push friends away by the way I work and pray. The world, and the dream, still until the will of all this fall crawl into how I fell into being well.

I almost want to close this Fountain here. I want to say that I've grown and that I have, and will have, known. I want to share the hearts of the world of Earth with many more than a few, and remind us that to God I owe full homage and devotion too. I also don't want to use, abuse, or lose you. I

103

almost typed that I didn't want to love. Love is a fragile dear and frightening thing. It's something that can chain a soul to nothing, even when that nothing feels like is a black hole to purge and cleanse and entrap my soul.

I pray well we carry on. We must.

I cannot tell you of all the love and loss. We know it deeper than many, though the depths of the plan and plot dig into our spirits, and also The Contialis.

I want to tell the story. It may be too soon, though. I also wish not to lose the chance to share. There's the case that we don't always know there is a tomorrow. For some people, they never reached today in life. Some are already gone. The wish and hope are others not forget; that we may remember them for the beauty and calamity of things we were never blessed enough to understand yet. That may be why they say 'they live in my heart.'

I don't want it to be over. It seems, in an odd way, that it's always often just near the beginning; that another grain of sand has landed in our hearts to be cultivated and tended. We dance and delve into the world with the delicate brilliance of a natural Sapphire. How could we ever be?

WHAT I'M DOING, AND WHY

Gary, you've helped me exceptionally. You may or may not know the effects of the lessons you've taught me, yet you may also say anything you want to. There are so many diverse people that you work with that are focal in your life. They also want to thrive, and I can comprehend how slackers like me cause you aggravation and agitation because you work so amazingly hard and well.

We also know that different people have different goals, wants, and objectives. Mine are so exceptionally basic. Learn, love, live, thrive, create, play and pray. These words are part of my prerogative, and you've helped fuel quite a few of them. I also trip myself up with the idea that you may not wish them on me too.

I already told you about the learn part; that you've taught me a lot of things that I may not have discovered on my own. Without a direct connection with you, you also remind me of the love part. The first keynote I saw of you was 'Care or Die.' I'm still trying to grasp that concept in my own heart and actions. From the #AskGaryVee show (episode 118) of you and your Dad, you reminded me that it is okay to love my Dad more than most anyone for now. The live part of the prerogative is shown in different ways and by understanding my qualities and needs.

I think of how you're in New York, and how I would have been destroyed many years ago if I lived in that eco-system. I gave a weak attempt at music and rapping in the previous city I lived in, and I now thoroughly know I'm not a rapper or an MC. One thing that you do, though, that I'd love to develop, is public speaking. You may not get nervous performing, though I'm a very insecure person sometimes, and I also have a layer of fear about being overconfident.

Your lessons in self-awareness are ideas I want to help others develop and share too. We know that by knowing ourselves, and what fuels our hearts, and minds, is what also guides us to do what we need to do. You want to own the Jets, and I contrarily haven't even been able to commit to Natalie. It comes from the point of my negative self-image and believing that I could never love her at all.

You grabbed hold and dominated your own will to be healthy too. You made a choice, you stuck with it, and you're now enjoying a full capacity of what it is to be you without so many contaminants. Your guidance leads to the fact that I don't want to be your Rick, and that I also don't understand how I can help you achieve your wants. The paranoid part of myself knows you are so much more hardcore business and life, and that there would maybe be no respect from you for a marshmallow like myself.

A layer of skepticism sometimes surrounds me. We are explicitly different humans, though that also means there are different parts of ourselves that others may try to poke and prod and disprove. In Daily Vee 80 there is a part where you were commanding your friend to make time to fly and meet you. Your passion, fire, and determination showed the full force that you love them so much that you were forcing them to make the connection.

FRAGMENTS OF INTENT

You speak of being agnostic, and you also said how when people make plans that God is to laugh. Twist back to #AskGaryVee episode 145 where you had D-Rock put a 'Reality Lord' graphic over top of yourself with thunderbolts and clouds. It's so rad and wonderful that you've given D-Rock, and so many others, the ability to have work that they can love too. You tend the soil of the gardens and fields you work for and with.

And, you're right, I don't think I've cared enough. I haven't had faith in my dreams, and I haven't let my heart draw forward what I want. I'm afraid it's not something I can achieve, yet you spoke of how regret is one of the worst things that we can have; we can't change it. My fear is, sometimes, that things will never change. I fear I'll not bring my courage forward to push for anything. I don't know how or if I'll quit the ciggies, and I'm concerned I'll keep wishing and waffling and not make a solid effort or take at earning a life I know I'll love.

You also spoke of how people should not be so concerned about what others think. The self-awareness layer twists in about how we also sometimes think of ourselves and how our views and assessments adjust who we are. My actions seem to tell me, and I partly agree, that I don't value myself.

I have communicated to some that I want to build other's lives and coach and mentor. My Glass House goal is to have a haven for people to spend half a week to a week in my home to build their dreams and to focus and gather for the work that they'll need to do. I want to earn the right to be the one that facilitates the seeds and the journeys, and maybe I'm passing the infant stages of the trip.

I remember that one is better than zero, and I hope to honour the rare few who talk with me. The idea of scarcity is not just about things, money, or valuable resources; it also applies to people. I think that my first want is to earn love, yet my self-reliance has lacked. I'd like to love and care for people, and that, from the four circles, is what the world needs. I need and value love for and from others, yet I too need to let others know they're also valued and appreciated.

You remind us to bank on our strengths, and you also tell us that EQ growth happens in a safer environment. I desire to have and hold and own my place as a safe environment so that I can grow with people. Of my strengths, I'm open to conversation with most people, and I believe in positive reciprocation. I also believe in giving and sharing, yet haven't had so much to share up to now. My fears of physical harm and people plotting are there sometimes, though if someone wants to communicate, I'm often open to that. With my reaching out to people, I also wish there be a purpose, which, yes, sometimes is just letting them know I like and care for them.

Writing to you is part of my process. I also don't know what I can give to you that would hold any value. I guess one thing is to buckle up and get serious about my work and get at it by putting myself and my work out there for others to see and learn. I'm still in the process of being less focused on my issues, and, yes, I still hopefully have a long way to go. When you talk about legacy, long-term, and the "you're going to die" comment, my insecurities must be set aside and send a wish and prayer to God and the universe. I will die, though many years, hopefully, decades, further in the future.

FRAGMENTS OF INTENT

I lack faith in myself. We also remember that some people may have faith in me. I'll not disappoint them. There is the idea of accountability to others, though I also must be accountable to myself. The push and pull of wanting to be purposed based are part of my motivations, and though I'm still so very young in my journey, I remember I shouldn't make comparisons to other people. Also noted, regarding self-awareness, I'm glad that I keep at it and learn. You've helped me with so many good seeds of this creation and intent, and you also tell your fans and followers that you intend to change lives. You do. I wish to also.

I'm not entirely sure what else to say to you for now. I want to quickly get this book done so that I can get it out there and get other works formed too. I am a 'book book' (a chicken joke) person and appreciate the idea of urgency. The desire is to share the book, and not for fear that I don't have time. I'm still astonished at the fact of how fortunate and lucky I am with the safety I receive. The grace of the world and the other forces of above and below help me make good of it.

I'm not out and set to meet you. I have no value to you that I'm aware of and note you're entangled with virtue too that some may not believe. The weaving of inspiration and the clear inhalation and exhalation of breath adds the last bit of this chapter to wish and pray. I ask we have decades further to live past this moment of time.

Grazie per nostra grazia sulla Terra; Italian for 'Thank you for our grace on Earth.' What if it all happened? For the super long term, I'll be there for my parents 90th birthdays and also wonder about the birth of my grandchildren. The Glass House will be a place where forty to fifty people will visit per year to focus on their lives, relationships, and businesses. Even if not my wife, I'll know and be able to talk with Natalie and have been able to learn, and continue to learn and share with others via book, internet, telephone, and direct visiting. I find and earn my Freedom Solution.

For the short term, like one year? I'll have found a way for my written and recorded work to support myself, so I'm not relying on parental or governmental funding. I'll have turned my home into a place where people like and love to gather, and I'll have started seeding dreams with other friends too. I'll have found myself to be a non-smoker or vape-only person, and if the ultimate ideas happen, I'll also have secured a chance to get put up on the tribal counsel shelf in the Survivor game and experience. Yes, I'm a dreamer.

For the long-term, performing lyrics is *not* something I want to do as a vocation. What about talking to groups of people as a public speaker though? It seems like a good idea, and the fear of being known by many people is one I held, though overcome. The gatherings for focus sessions are an idea I'd like to happen, and I find others that are future sighted. I also, hopefully, find my soulmate. With what I've said I want in my life up to now, those are things that I'm more confident of now, even if I think I'm foolish for thinking so.

For others, what do you want in your life? What is your ideal situation for a year from now? For ten years from now? What are some things you can do to get to work on those things today? What behaviours do you want to adjust, change, or fortify? What are some things that you can use for your foundational structure? Is it that you value what you can do (skills and abilities), who you know (current, past, or

FRAGMENTS OF INTENT

future relationships), or even your attitude (support and encouragement)? What if you can combine them?

At the start of the 2nd Fountain, I had a question: "So Rob, is this a life-coaching book, the story of you and Natalie, or just you thinking you have something to share? What this turned into is a web of a few of those things. I developed a reverence for God, I adjusted some behaviours, and I reminded myself of some things that I had forgotten. I share more of my thoughts and Introversial codes, though the main thing is to expand awareness; of ourselves, our world(s), and our values.

We learn. We love. We live. We thrive. We create. We play. And some of us also pray.

Keep your being open to the journey!

ROBERT KOYICH

TO THE ORIGINAL LOVESTONE

I cannot claim that I wrote this for just you. It's a journey of being that I need to fragment, scatter, and hone. Though I use you as the contialitic and soulful cleat for this chapter, you will probably not see what I've written. It's perhaps that only a few others that read this, yet I could be wrong.

I had an idea to use this as a testament to past loves and friends that were known before I left Edmonton. Ignoring what happened after SFU, some should not yet be revealed. Some before would say I can't even love or that I'm just another actor playing a part. My obsessive nature carries forward with layers and ideas of what I thought, including a few for whom I cared for and still care.

I'm still finding my path to real connection. Though I don't yet know the one I grow old with, some key people help form me. You, Thea, were the one that I thought I loved before finding and falling for Natalie.

In the first two books, I referred to a spiritual relic that I had that was a stone I called the Metamorphic Heart. The rock was in the shape of a heart, though had a corner broken off. I found the relic in a stone circle cast on a forest path near the townhouses at SFU where I broke the stone circle. I kept the Metamorphic Heart. I've not known if you cast the stone circle I broke, though I note you were Wiccan, so it very well could have been your circle.

I used the Metamorphic Heart as a metaphor for my heart.

The full stone represented my heart being for Natalie, the True Lovestone, with the corner broken off symbolizing you, Thea, as the Original Lovestone. You were the first one that I used to think and believed I loved. Teal, my girlfriend in high school, might not like that, yet she also seemed to intuit in that I didn't know back then how to care so much.

I'm not sure that I'd yet known or grown the ability to care and honour another person those many years ago. I've been, even recently, too self-focused and partly isolated. Through much of my life, I've lived in some precise amounts of fear, even if not only from my schizophrenic diagnosis. I think about Ryan Jackson and how he had called me 'Rob, the schizophrenic MC' and want to write to him too, even if not in this book. The ability to love is the one thing I want to foster, curate, develop and discover fully.

The years of obsession, delusion, and infatuation for some gals have been with me since the point of when you and I last spoke. We lost our contact between in 1998-1999 when I was brought back to Edmonton to the psych ward. I know I had lost you some time before then, though poetically, it seems that I shed some layers of my heart many years before knowing how to start.

I've not forgotten about you, though, or some of the other friends that I'll write to and about. I've not forgotten the mistakes I made that showed a lack of respect, yet also know I did and do honour you in some ways. I don't know if I was welcome or not, though the way I've told the story to some doesn't make sense to me either; there are discrepancies about timelines in my course of life.

FRAGMENTS OF INTENT

Was it your stone circle that I broke to steal the Metamorphic Heart? You were Wiccan, and I know your spirituality focuses on such things as rituals, stones, and magic. The stone park I built where the first circle broke was torn down in reciprocation. My intent held to guard the new ring as an overseer, and I had gone back to the path on SFU campus to see where the lovestone city and park had been. That area had been torn apart years later by heavy machinery.

I didn't know back then in 1996 that you would become one of the first girls that I'd get over-focused on and obsessed. I rewind to when we first met and how you already had a boyfriend. I had lacked basic decency, and I don't think I fully understood that you were loyal to him. I won't reveal your secrets, though know that I remember how I breached the touch-line boundaries after we smoked our first joint in our first weeks of knowing each other.

My drug life at SFU is a time that I call my 'happy-hippy-fun days.' The interactions and people on SFU campus were with so many rad and eclectic people that had their own kind and trippy lives going on. A lot of those people knew how much I was on about you back then, and I think of people like Crazy Mike and Matt X knowing about my infatuation with you. I can almost hear their advice to just chill. SFU was an epic saga, though. "Sooo cinematic!"- Dave Clark.

I had two other drug lives after we met. I went back to Edmonton to Grey Nun's hospital after SFU and spent a while in the psych ward. I don't know how long I was there, though it was winter, and I was released in 1999. It was after my first trip to the hospital that I got involved in street life. It was not happy-hippy-fun days like SFU, though I called myself a cyber hippy. After a summer of being a Twinkie (a person who hangs out with street people, though lives with their parents) I was kicked out of my mom's home for bringing street people over.

Even now, two decades after you and I first met, I can recall how badly I fell for you. Later in my life, I started to focus on Natalie, and even though I've claimed Natalie is a partial source of my mental illness, that, maybe, isn't entirely true. It was the drugs and my experiences even *before* Natalie where I started to get messed up substantially. Drugs were not the pathway to divinity for me as some think they can be.

I'm sad that I lost you, though I hope you are living happily now. You had cared for me and my infantile heart so well, and it seemed like you were following what you thought *you* needed to do. Hooking up with me was at the whim and wish of others and not your own heart. I thought that you were going to give your body up to me, though I sensed you didn't want to, so kept myself from doing so. It's where I've thought I loved you more than a physical relationship and had respected you. I don't know what your honest wants were, or if you were meant to be a sacrificial offering.

I only hold *some* visual recollections of my past before the year 2000. They are just little guidance as to what I have forgotten. The people that I want to write to are different points of care from friendship and relationship, and it is true a few of them knew each other. You, though, Thea, were one of the first that I thought I loved.

I want to break past some of my fears about loving and caring. I've gotten obsessed and over-focused on some

FRAGMENTS OF INTENT

people while neglecting others. I yet learn how to appreciate another for who and what they are, instead of how I like them, or even my gain from the friendship. Some friends from the far distant past hold stories of their own that I may not receive the blessing of knowing. If this Fountain was meant to be about my heart and the friendships and connections that help and have helped form me, then I saw you, Thea, the one with whom to start.

Why is it I have gotten so obsessed with some people? Why have I seemed to fall into infatuation instead of tending dear hearts with reasonable care? Why have I been so money focused and not having faith that I'll earn my life? How can I learn to dream and share, learn, and teach how to love? How can I free myself of the shackles and chains that have held me back from really loving life and being exceptionally glad to live?

I am alone. I accept that. I also note that there are some that visit from time to time. It's been almost 17 years since I left Vancouver to where I live now. So much life occurs that seems to only hint at the inner journey my being's experiences. I've formed some written work, and recorded music, though, after the 17 years in this town, I don't seem to understand yet how I can, and hopefully shall get another 17 years further into the future. I note, though, that the chains of Natalie are not quite so tight about my being.

I hope you have found your spouse, Thea. I hope you allowed yourself the beauty and brilliance of children. I recall how kind and real you were and knew you'd be a blissful and loving mother and wife. You were so beautiful, groovy, and kind and such a dear gal that I shouldn't have put myself towards. I heard from Jesse Itzler about 'the right girl at the right time' being the principal idea.

You may not have been the right girl, and it's clear that I focused on you at the wrong time. You had a boyfriend when I moved on you, and you made the correct choice to leave the room and not engage. I know it was a transgression I cannot change, and in life now, I remind myself to fortify bonds with couples; to strengthen their relationships, honour them, and be one to ensure they hold more strong and true.

I've so often found myself, and my lessons, in life as being after the point of mistake. I've not commonly understood in advance the consequence of my actions. I'm still flawed and so often overthinking about my crack thoughts and errors, and I want not to do that; I'd like to be kind or helpful to others and their goodness. I've tried to create purpose and value in and of myself without fully recognizing that I still can be too selfish. Teal knew that back when she and I were a couple in high school.

You remind me I have a story, though. My memory tells me that I've often wanted a relationship with a gal a bit too strongly at times. Maybe it's the years of my depravity that keep me from having a girlfriend. Over the past few years, I've often said: "I can't even afford me, let alone a girlfriend." And there is truth to that too. I've held beliefs that my wrong actions are partly the cause of my lack because if I'm not behaving correctly, then I seem to believe I should not receive prosperity. It's my intuition and idea that we also *do* get what we deserve.

There's the belief that people who are prosperous earn it, and

FRAGMENTS OF INTENT

I may not have been doing the correct things for myself to allow love either. Others may not agree with me that those with much have earned it, though I note I also haven't heeded too well to some other people's opinions.

I feel remorse for how I've been sometimes. Not just with you, Thea, though also with how I've travelled so many years and still feel like I've brought myself up to the point of being a nihilist. I have called out to God, and I know people hold extreme value. I still, though, am isolated and too self-focused to find that maybe there is a world for which I'm to be integrated. I have, in the past, heard people say I try too hard and that I'm impatient and pushing the process.

I also add, now, that I knew so very little about you. I could tell you about what I thought about you, though how I felt to know you makes me recall how saddening it was to lose you. The facts of *who* you are and were have not been forgotten to the sands of time. You, Thea, I think were the first girl that I loved. It reminds me of how unhealthily obsessive I can be when I fall for a girl.

Regarding other parts of my life, I still am an addict. I may not be drinking lots of alcohol or smoking dope (or needles or sniffles) though my addiction to cigarettes is also a profound dirty thing. I had the thought the other day about cigarettes being 'an income inhibitor.' Tobacco is a drug that I've relied heavily upon since I was in high school, and I don't yet have an entire understanding of the psychological reasons for my addiction. I want to find the source.

Why did and didn't I respect your boundaries? For what was I even searching? What was it that brought you to want to interact with me? What happened to you? If you were the one gal that was my first love and infatuation, from where had my obsessive nature stemmed?

I know I'm very neurotic and insecure sometimes. I know there are lots of fragments and shards of despair in my being. I'm afraid of what's within me. I have an intuition that there are so many points of filth and obsessive waste embedded in my nature, and I want to heal and cleanse these things. Bringing them up and then setting them free through the keys is part of the process that lets me become aware, acknowledge, and accept them, though if there are pieces of myself I dislike, I want not to suppress them. I want to admit, process, and change them, so they don't fester further. Writing for me is a healing process.

I don't know if there ever was a 'right time' with you, or even if you could have been 'the right girl.' I know too that I could probably never have been the 'right guy.' Writing of my past will find some good things.

I may not be able to talk with you or some of the people that I write to, though my memories pluck some points of awareness. I wonder if it's worth divulging my aspects of angst and abomination to find shreds of divine goodness and gladness. I hope so. We shall discover.

I'M AN ADDICT

Okay, this is becoming a bit clearer; the facts of this book dredge up some of my faults and emotional shrapnel. I wanted to write chapters out to different people from my past and did so by writing to Thea. This chapter I wanted to write to Brent, though the situation I was in with my cigarettes guided me to write this chapter outwards and not to one specific person. I'm not sure if I should even write out to Brent because that's a story and history that's not mine alone to share.

The issue that guided the title of this chapter is the topic of smoking cigarettes. When I wrote the chapter to Thea, it dredged up reminders of how I've been emotionally unhealthy and obsessive. With my financial lack over the past few years, I became quite conscious of my obsessive nature with my addiction to tobacco.

I've referred to being shackled to some things, and we've known how I chain myself to things and people. In the past, we know how explicitly obsessed with Natalie I was, and I didn't, before starting the 3rd Fountain, recall how obsessive I was with Thea too. My mental and emotional health issues go back a long time, and I think the drug use influenced my derailment from a decent life. It's tricky to get back on the tracks. It was during high school that I first dabbled with marijuana, though this chapter is not about the illegal drugs I smoked either.

I know I'm an addict with how my behaviour has been through the three to five days before writing this. I had no pouch, tin, or pack of smokes, and still, I scrounged up some fragments of tobacco to smoke. I went through almost all of my cigarette butts, fished pieces of tobacco from my office garbage can, and even found two or so smokes from the grains that fell into my computer keyboard.

The chemicals that I smoke and drink now (ciggies and coffee) are legal drugs, though legality is not the issue. The mental and theoretical physical dependency that I have with coffee and cigarettes are *not* something I like. I chose not to smoke drugs (meth, marijuana, coke) and have kept to that since 2004. The cigarettes and coffee, though, are still a vice upon my being.

In November 2016, I committed to going 24 hours without a cigarette. I maintained my promise, though with five to seven hours before the 24 hours were complete, I was getting very edgy and pissed off. When the clock reached 12:42 AM, the end of the 24 hours, I soon after lit up a rolled smoke. Other than those 24 hours, I've maybe only once or twice gone that long without smokes since high school.

When I first typed this section, I was without ciggies with no clue as to where I could get some. A different issue arises when having a lack of cigarettes; the concept of sminking. Sminking is a word that I stole from my mom's friend Gloria many years ago. Gloria used the word as a combination of the words smoking and drinking and used the word about how she didn't like her son 'sminking.' I later took the word and used the term as a way to describe the mooching of cigarettes.

FRAGMENTS OF INTENT

If I'm to write a different book to help guide people, then I need to sort out myself so that I can guide others. I could give lots of advice or information about what I have done from knowing what is not good, though I need to find my positive solutions and share them. I've made some progress with my independence, though I'm not there yet with living an entirely healthy life.

The idea is we must first become aware of things, acknowledge them, and then thirdly accept them. Within my smoking process, I am aware I'm deeply addicted, I recognize it (to others and myself), and I accept it. I don't like that I'm addicted, though acknowledge and agree that for now, I'm a smoker.

I want to remind us to build ourselves up. So often I've spoken very negatively to and of myself, and I've made comments about 'the kid in the mirror.' Sometimes I've sworn at my reflection when displeased with how I've been, and I also note that the person in the mirror sometimes has that silly smile on their face. I'm glad they talk to me sometimes too!

For building myself up, I should remind myself that I have made it through breaking the marijuana and illicit chemical habits. A friend commented about my sobriety yesterday and asked how I have done it. I need to remind myself of how I have gone fourteen plus years without puffing on a joint even if I do love green. There are two primary reasons, and a third, as to why I don't smoke drugs anymore.

The first two reasons why I don't smoke drugs anymore are my parents and my mental health. I've made the joke that if I ever puffed again, that I'd immediately teleport. It's also partly fear that keeps me from drugs. I can imagine what would happen to me if I ever drugged again, and the fear of what would happen helps fortify my resolve. As I typed this paragraph, I could feel the anxiety and fear in my stomach that reminds me that I'm afraid I'd puff again.

If I ever smoked a joint again, I believe I'd land back in the psych ward. I don't want to go there again. I think of how my parents would disown me, and they are two of the most valuable people for me in my life. I have no brothers or sisters, and without my parents, I don't have many strong connections with many other family members.

Maintaining I don't smoke drugs is a commitment made to my parents and myself, and the fear of the consequences of what would happen if I ever did again keeps me from doing so. One other key point is even if marijuana's legal, it's still *not* okay for me to smoke green.

The ciggies are part of my current life situation. I hope and pray that they are not guaranteed to be a full lifelong entrapment. I don't know how to quit, and I also don't have enough future sight to think of the long-term points of my life. There have been times where I've feared getting killed, and have thought that I enjoy smoking. If ciggies would not be the cause of my death, then why take away that pleasure? I do want of a long life, though I may be in denial about how I may live another few decades to the point where smoking would be the reason for shortening my life.

I am, perchance, too present based and hedonistic. I have thought of doing what I like regarding consuming (e.g.

smoking and coffee) and haven't enough faith or care for how they affect me. If I do want to live a long life, then it seems contradictive to be a smoker.

We also know and should remind ourselves that chemical habits are not the only type of addictions that people have. Some people are addicted to working, some are addicted to sex, and some are addicted to exercise and obsessed with health. Some are addicted to gambling, and some are addicted to retail therapy or buying things.

With the nicotine fits I had in the last week of November 2016, I found I have a thick layer of hating myself sometimes. I learned at PD Seminars that addiction can be a cover for a self-hate cycle and that the dependencies are used to hide that. With the first 3A's (Aware, Acknowledge, Accept) I now know more clearly that there are some layers of self-hate and dissatisfaction with myself from time to time. I'd found myself verbally saying "I smoke cigarettes, so I don't want to kill myself" with the cigarettes used as a distraction. Cigarettes pacify and help calm some of my negative feelings about myself.

I *have* broken the addiction to buying Magic cards, I *have* maintained my commitments to sobriety, and I did make it through 24 hours without smoking. These three things remind and blend into me an idea that I can commit to other choices to reduce my intake. There are many positive things to be gained by quitting, though I still haven't made a decision. I must garner the courage required to stop. My lack of faith and fear of a non-smoking future is also a part of this.

If you are a smoker (or another type of addict), maybe it's a good idea to get more conversations formed about the addiction. I believe that talking about problems is a way to resolve them. If we have discussions about *why* we do what we do, we may dig deeper. We may find the causational or trigger points and then lead back to parts about ourselves that we don't like and heal them.

Maybe *that's* a Natalie thing!?! That I hate myself, and my lack of resources, and that a magical beauty would swoop in and steal me away from a life I sometimes don't like? The idea of being 'saved' by another person would 'fix' my situation and bring me into a positive future? That's a different topic, though, and not about addiction. It may link to self-worth, and why we have the situations we have. We often get what we think we deserve.

I like the chemical pleasure of cigarettes, and when I have enough resources to smoke, I'm glad to have them. I wonder what would happen if I got obsessed about my health? Some people say that to drop one addiction that we need to take up another. I've noticed when focused in and on my work that I sometimes won't break from the computer. I don't want to replace one addiction with another. What is this internal system of reward and want that keep us chained to things? I'm not sure that I know right now… maybe it's best to return to this later.

In *Searching for Tomorrow* and also *Shared Node,* I conveyed some of the Survivor dream and ideas. I wrote about how I gave a challenge to Jeff Probst to accept the challenge of quitting smoking to compete on Survivor. I maintain the commitment to stop if given a chance to compete, yet also wonder if I'd return to the habit after the season. I don't know, and since I'm Canadian, I couldn't play yet according to previous rules. Maybe we shall see.

I sometimes love the lungfuls of smoke. It's not a good thing, though, and I know that from a few points. I'll never recommend smoking to another, and I'm conscious that it's not a good habit to have for others to see me have. I want to be a good example, and if I do move forward as a role model, then I want to live ethically and honourably. I don't see smoking as something I'd ever promote or want to seed for another's life. I also think of how people may not want to support me if I'm a smoker. I found a statement in the past week; that I want my work to have value, purpose, and meaning for others, and not just use them just for my monetary gain.

Then too, if I speak of the things I like about smoking, there's a teetering point of sharing my honest truths without seeding potential negative behaviours. I'd prefer to have a positive effect, though I also want to tear myself apart and rebuild without some of the wrong things. If I value radical honesty and writing about my faults is therapeutic, then should I dredge up all my thoughts about smoking? Maybe.

There is a spiritual component with smokes too. I draw and learn some truth from ciggies, and depending on when I take a pull of a cigarette, or if I tap the smoke, or even how my thoughts are when I spark or extinguish a cigarette, I know that ciggies are a communication tool too. Is this why some people are social smokers?

There are opinions from others that smoking is terrible, and

I've also written that if I'm one who values and wants to create and support life. It seems contradictory that I smoke; especially when I get it's such an awful thing for my health. Even in the Magic code cigarettes are 'black' mana symbolizing death and decay. I think I've been conditioned and told by so many people that smoking is wrong, that I almost want to argue that.

By always having enough tobacco, I've thanked God for letting me have enough nicotine. Even the previous week, when I was scraping out every source of tobacco in my home to smoke, I found a way. Smokers are resourceful. I wonder what would happen if I gave thanks to God for every cigarette? I instinctively think that I'd intuit that God doesn't want me to smoke, and I wonder how I'd respond to that spiritual component.

A few years ago, I wrote a list of fifteen or so excellent reasons to quit smoking, and each one is exceptionally valid. There are many benefits to being a non-smoker. The hedonistic and present based pleasure part of myself seems to hold the habit with more strength. With the 24 hours I went without smoking, I knew very clearly I wanted to smoke before the 24 hours were up. To give up the habit *forever* will not be easy.

For my mind (learning), my soul and spirit (health), and even my prosperity (money), I want to be a healthier person. I believe in incremental improvement, and I read once about tennis. If a player wins 55% of their games (first six games win the set, three of five sets wins the match), the results are tremendous! (Think also of Anthony Robbins and compounded interest). If I can start winning my internal

FRAGMENTS OF INTENT

battles for the future, allow myself to believe long-term, and make many incremental advantages, maybe I can and shall start making some drastic changes.

Anyhow, let's break for now. From where I was when I started this chapter, I know I'm addicted still. I also know that I feel inspired to make changes and refine my life as being many parts, and not just the ciggies. Even if they've consumed me sometimes, I must move forward and make small motions towards who I want to be; even if not for Natalie like some years had called me. We find the synergy of what I do for who we are to be.

Orbiting around a star like the tar bars that burn, I learn to develop and adjust. Rob, trust in yourself to keep yourself held on the shelf. Even if you need to improve your health, the wealth of time and attitude shift into how we're inclined to allude to another twist to assist the gift. She shall lift her eyes into the creative reprise, even if you think you're both only lies.

ROBERT KOYICH

CONTINUE TO LEARN

I think of how this book, like *Shared Node*, could include a glossary, though I've not used so many new words. I've now formed the main base of this book, and I like the idea of including this as a title to sell on Amazon. Though the first three books merged into the full form of this book, the process of writing is good for me and my well-being. I learn a lot about myself writing the Fountains books, and I also know I have a great deal more to learn, share, and write. I've learned that I've made a lot of personal progress and that I can't just magically 'fix' other people or situations.

A significant portion of my learning and development occurred in the time since I released the first book. Though most of my stories go back much further into the past, the damage and neurosis in my being *are* clearing. My intents and behaviours are continuing to change, and I can see some mistakes that I've made through the years. Even if I *have* changed and grown through the past years, it's not readily known of or comprehended by many of my contacts. I've not spoken with lots of them recently, and I've lacked friends that I can talk with about my work and progress. I *am* open to feedback. However, I need to develop my openness and understanding further.

The most significant thing that I've learned since the first book is that I'm still very flawed *and* willing to work towards the future. I've pushed out past from the Natalie dream, and I'm terrified that I still could be secretly chained to her by the fact that I've also neglected the idea. I don't like quitting or giving up on things. I've learned how I'd been entirely unhealthy with Natalie and Thea, and maybe that's the reason I cast aside signs and wonders that point to them and some others. Some songs, poets, and even Wayne and Garth said that "if you let her go, and she comes back to you, then it was meant to be."

That leads to another skill I'm developing; to be hopeful and optimistic about an outcome, yet also to be glad about a different result. Coles Books was reviewing a copy of *Shared Node* to decide if they would sell the books at their store. I prepared myself for both potential situations. If they said 'yes,' then I'd be glad to have a book signing and have books sold there, yet I also knew that if they didn't accept the book that I'd have the eight copies to share with others. They chose not to carry the book, and I was okay with that.

With the snow shovelling during winter 2016-2017, I used the same technique. At the point of the snow stopping for a bit, that meant either a) the snow would return, and we'd work later (more money) or b) we'd get to go home (sleep and relaxation). I think that is a crucial idea and lesson to share with people; to be hopeful and glad about any outcome. Another concept from Stephen Covey's book *The Seven Habits of Highly Effective People* of 'the third option' reminds that if we have two options and are not okay with either, to find the third. The central premise, though, is to prepare to be glad no matter what happens.

I've also learned more about my purpose and the functions of what I've formed up to now. A rare friend gave me the idea to form a blurb or description of the works that I've made or

FRAGMENTS OF INTENT

am making. I've not explicitly stated what the books are, though share here some of the relevance.

The Fountain Books:

> The Fountain Series is a series of books that track the journey, growth, and development of myself and my work. I use the books as a way to share, learn, process, and accept my inner self. The series started as a way to connect and heal some of my emotional and mental damage, though the audience for the books are those interested in who I am, what I have been through, and how I work to achieve a cohesive, harmonious, and prosperous future.

Shared Node:

> *Shared Node* is a creative lyrical formation of a style of rhyming called flowetics. The book evolves through manual reviews adjusting the threads of extended thought. The book's source files were from pages of rhyme I had written to individual people (both known, and unknown) and carry wishes and undercurrents of life through the reader's comprehension. *Shared Node* is meant to be read for entertainment and as a different way to play with reality. It uses some ideas and language that formed during my drug lives and psychosis.

Beautiful, Do You Mind?:

> *Beautiful, Do You Mind?* is written to include ideas about relationships and communicate an understanding of love. The work is also meant to be a way to play with reality and go on a shared

journey. Though the Fountains books track my process and evolution, *Beautiful, Do You Mind?* carries more of my stories, beliefs, and opinions about how we are on Earth. The book's audience is for both genders and is meant to link with telepathy.

Built from Within:

Built from Within is about communication, creation, and interpersonal understanding. The work includes theories about life in community and connection with a twist of what divides and unites us. The discussions partly are how bridging together differing viewpoints in a shared world is vital. It includes topics of religion, psychosis, and otherworldly and dream experiences; different perspectives about our multiple forms of 'self.'

May this be part of the structure I need to move forward? I'm glad my parents have been so dearly supportive of me, and I wish others to have great parents too. I hope we can be accepted to make our own choices and mistakes and have criticism and judgment suspended. It allows a level of freedom to learn and heal.

As my Mom's started to be less critical and less judgmental, I've been less fearful of telling her about parts of my life. My Mom and I's relationship and openness to communication have improved a lot, and I feel sad a bit that *I* haven't loved her so much more honestly in the past. I'm glad she's allowed me to form my path, even if I'm a muddle, not a muggle.

My Dad is one who's given me lots of advice through the

FRAGMENTS OF INTENT

years, though he too has been less critical and more accepting. My parents are, at this point in our relationships, showing me a lot of crucial behaviours, actions, and attitudes that I appreciate. Although I barely believe I'll ever be a parent, a lot of their examples affect how and what I'll teach to my kids.

On a scale of 1-10 of how happy I am with my sight towards the future? I put it as a five. My lack of faith is what keeps it from a seven or eight. I've lacked confidence, though knowing that can give me a push to ask for more from myself. To lift my future to an 8-10 will be earned over the next five years with the foundational work done in the formation of these books.

I learn to seek my inner guidance, I learn to ask more valuable questions, and I learn how to suspend my voice to hear from others. I also learn to relax and trust a clean breath now and then. I learn how to set aside my wants and intents and tend to others, and I've learned that I don't want to be an MC and perform. I hone my craft and my abilities to write as a skill and tool I can use for others.

I learn to be more patient, to be kind to myself, and to allow myself grace to create; like staying up late to work. I also remember to stop myself from making poor choices. The night I wrote this I was in bed at 3-4 AM (because of shovelling snow until 3 AM) though I think, right now, that I should sign off and get to bed. I have read and understood the idea of forming good habits, though it's self-discipline, like language lessons and reading, that can help fortify a positive future.

It *was* the next day from the previous paragraph before I got back to this. I was up and out of bed early and spent an hour reading *The Success Principles* by Jack Canfield before returning to this chapter. The book *The Success Principles* is an *amazing* one. If you want to improve your life, please get a copy of Jack's book! It will bolster your faith in yourself and your process drastically. It's a valuable read for your future.

Three main ideas I need to heed from *The Success Principles* are:

- To accept full responsibility for my life (It's all because of ourselves, our choices, and our actions).

- Criticism and negative feedback can be more valuable than positive feedback.

- Choosing to do things each day towards our goals compounds our confidence in them.

Lewis Howes, I thank you for your podcast, books, lessons and love too! Your podcast is how I found Jack, and even if you're not to read *this* book, open admiration to you for performing your mission and vision; to inspire one hundred million people to make a full-time living doing what they love. Even if I'm not there yet, I'll keep at it!

I learn more about people both known and unknown, my perceptive abilities increase, and my patience and compassion grow. These assist me to understand behaviours of myself as well as others. I continue to cultivate my humility, my awareness, my joy (crucial), and know I can care and love more than I used to. I'm practicing and allowing myself to choose how and who I'll permit to be in my life, and some people, even if not by their intent, are *not* suitable for me and

FRAGMENTS OF INTENT

my life. The lesson is we're allowed to limit and also shut out the involvement of negativity in our lives. Even if people have positive and good intentions, sometimes they're people from whom we best stay away.

Accusations by others can cloud with projected beliefs. Negativity and judgment are real things, and through other's viewpoints, they aren't always accurate about the truths of ourselves. Theorizing about other's intents isn't always right. We can ask people the question: "what do you think?" and "why do you think that?" to help gain clarity when we need to. Self-awareness is a vital thing, and I remind myself to check other's opinions and feedback with my truths. What another thinks is good for us may not be in reality.

Give yourself the space to explore negative feedback and check it with yourself too. Openness is a vital thing, though be not swayed away from your truths and core being if you are sure of them.

I just had a feeling similar to where *Searching for Tomorrow* closed; the pull of energy that makes me want to be done with this book and onto the next. I *could* draw into that action now and close this book immediately. My intuitive guidance instills the idea that there is an urge to share this work with the world. The saying "The world isn't ready for me yet" holds on, yet that's because I know it may take a few years to solidify the grip and tracks of my journey. The feeling and urge to birth books is one I learn to manage, though it gives me a sign that I'm hopefully on the right course and path.

How shall we close this book? I thought to complete more in

this book, review, edit, process, and release, though these are *The Fountains of Yesterday*. The next series of these books is *The Fountains of Faith; The Second Three Fountains*.

If *Fragments of Intent* is the result of the first three Fountains books, and the second three compile to *The Sands of Yesterday*, what will the future works be? If you're reading this, you'll have access to the Fountains *Etched in Stone* and *Open to Fate* too, though the three-part *Shards of My Soul* wasn't yet ready.

So, as of right now, the intent? Finish this book, release it, and find ways of getting more copies into readers hands, eyes, and hearts!

Love, light, luck, and life! I pray you full wellness of being too; we continue our lives.

ANOTHER FRAGMENT OF INTENT

Okay, back to January 29th, 2017. I became aware of the audiences for the book work. The Fountains books have a limited and open audience that are the people interested or intrigued by me, my long-term story, or our process. Though that audience is tiny at this point, it's good to know. If you are reading this book, you've given me a great gift in making an effort (or having the interest) in following my journey. I also know that with such a small audience, that I perchance should not focus too much. The books add depth to life and the world by forming and sharing them, though I've not adulted well.

Earlier when finishing the 3rd Fountain, I met with a friend at my home for our first focus session. By the end of the meeting, we had set five goals each to accomplish by the next meeting two weeks later. We met the following week again and had made progress. We set another four to five things to complete before our next meeting, and although I made forward motion, the items almost became a task list. It made me think of a comment from a past friend "progress, not perfection." The four goals/tasks that I set resulted in getting a chapter written, expanding my goals, and plans to achieve those goals.

It brought me back to the idea of the combination of love, work, and effort towards solutions, and not just checking off items on a list. Some people have said that if we're doing what we want to do and are happy that that's winning. Is it as simple as that? One's Freedom Solution is being able to do what we want to do, with who we want to do it, and also when and where we want to do it (and with full financial support).

My task list would say that I need to be working on *Fractured Formation*, though I don't want to push or force the process. Getting things done is crucial, though if doing things because we *have* to, not *want* to, may result in sub-par work or product. Inspiration should, I think, not be forced. I believe there's value in setting goals and committing to working towards them, though the process also includes being happy to be doing what we are to do to achieve our future.

I may be too accepting and not pushing well enough for the future that I want. The level of knowledge I have holds a decent situation, though perhaps I strive for an even better one. Maybe my mind and attitude are off and askew for not setting higher expectations for myself and what I want to do and be. I don't want just to be scattering seeds to the wind. I want to grow things and cultivate growth in our lives, our gardens, and also help others tend their lives too! I've said I want to plough the fields for combined yields, yet maybe I am sowing the wrong seeds.

Twenty-four hours later, I resumed.

Though I'm not financially secure or stable when I write this, I have made some good progress. The fact I'm not living a sufficiently stable and robust financial life reminds me that I have further to go before sharing a lot of life advice. I need to learn and develop before I can write books that will give a structured guideline about how to be prosperous. I've not

FRAGMENTS OF INTENT

figured it out yet, and note I have heard the advice that we need to know and find our stability before supporting others. If people blend into my life and process as we see our paths and futures, we work alongside each other towards prosperity.

I have passed from being a psych ward patient to living in a group home to having my apartment and a full-time job. Even if I fell away from being able to handle full-time work, I've passed quite a few checkpoints. I may not be a professional expert, though I've gained a lot of experience with life through my recovery. While I can't quite be a business or relationship expert by experience, I have some knowledge and advice that can help some other people closer to the beginnings of their journeys.

Insert another four days between sections.

I slept well last night. I had been shovelling snow for the three days previous (77cm fell within 72 hours), and it was a great thing for me. The money I earned could be used to repay my savings, though money issues have hounded me, even when not my own. I was to make contact with a friend that I've had problems with through the years, though I'm not clear how to convey to them my viewpoint. Perchance they might not understand my position.

Because it was snow removal for the previous three days, and potentially that day and the next, I hadn't focused on book work or future planning. I printed two documents of life goals, and I remind myself to review them more often. Some of my goals seem quite outlandish right now, though linked from Christy Whitman I shall set my intent and align with my higher purpose. I found that the Seed Funds are still a strong idea, and there is truth I'll work well with them. I also want to process more in conversation, not just typing, about how the funds will be used. I want to ensure they are a benefit, and not seen as a mooch point.

I was into chapter eight of *The School of Greatness*, by Lewis Howes and want to get further into *The Success Principles* by Jack Canfield too. I remind myself that books are a way to grow, process, and track our journeys. Even if I don't sell insane amounts of copies of this or the other Fountains books, I shall work with them towards our future.

Add a few hours between paragraphs

I completed chapter eight of *The School of Greatness* and the conclusion. Thank you, Lewis! I'll want to read the book through again, and one of my goals to learn more. I have a long-term goal of reading 500 or more books by the time the Glass House is built. The home's library shall include a few many I've already read through the past few years.

The School of Greatness reminded me that my intents and ideas of wanting to give back to the world need not be only monetary. For some friends, I've not been happy with them asking for resources, though I can give to them by being a different kind of support. I can help them by being a friend even if not to provide them with money or cigarettes.

Introversial isn't very marketable at this point, though I also don't diminish the worth and abstract quality it and its work holds. Though I'm not following standard patterns or templates for my creative work, that's where I also don't want to abuse the creative freedoms I've often held.

FRAGMENTS OF INTENT

This book was available as individual items, though I redid the books and merged them into *Fragments of Intent*. The first three Fountains twisted in and up and mixed in many changes, shifts, and turns between sentences and thoughts. We wove this tapestry after I removed some chapters and more than two-thirds of the third Fountain in the final version.

I'll write more books, though please forgive me for shifting and zigging and zagging so much. Though I want to be a set, solid, real and fortified Shoulsman, the flux and variations of my text and thought are like Ashley's tattoo, a dandelion. I had the idea to give some precursor in this book about the next projects, though one thing at a time.

How can I be such a waffle using secret tactics while also so overtly and neurotically revealed? Things hidden in the midden of my work find I could explain all of my secrets to the world, though, should I be so open? I'd like to have nothing to hide, so must reveal my feelings and reactions to some things. Some may not like that I talk about them in a book though, so there's a twist of releasing books that may have a wide audience even if they're all about me and my life.

There's a delicate balance of sharing the whole ball of wax, and also keeping respect for others and their privacy. I heed their feelings and their beings and by talking so much about the things in my life, does that shield them too? If I'm absorbed in my life and process, does that neglect sharing other people's debris? My Dad would say I've shared way too much about myself, though I blend to be wary of consequences. Perhaps a teetering balance also allows wisdom.

Wisdom: The quality of having experience, knowledge, and good judgment; the quality of being wise.

So here we are at the end of the book. Although the final version was after the release of the next few Fountains, I am glad you came back to read into it. My life and work balances with points of care and commitment, and though the results weren't clear to me, some nudges and inklings reminded me that this is good work.

Writing the base text of my books is sometimes more difficult than the editing process. With the editing, though, I don't always know or understand when a book is done. When do I free them to the world in their final form? It's like letting a prayer go out knowing the wishes and intents, yet forgetting what I asked for in the prayer. That is where I must trust my intentions, energies, and karma to allow the best results manifest.

If you have gained from this book, I appreciate such, and if you read this book, you have given a great gift. Thank you for helping me tend my gardens of heart and for helping provide. I'd love to know and meet the Glass House and my future family, and I send this wish outwards through text.

Keep myself in line with what is best for yourself. I may not go out to search for Natalie, though she is where my written journey started. Perhaps she does know who I am, and on the chance that she doesn't, and my belief of a spiritual connection was a delusion, it would be nice to tell her "thank you for love" and let her live her life.

145

146

ACKNOWLEDGMENTS

I thank all forces of life, truth, and creative instinct, I thank God and The Universe for allowing us continued grace, and I thank my friends, family, and community for allowing me to create these books.

My Mom, my Dad, and my step-parents have helped me so much through the course of my life. I wish to return the favour of love and support to them too. My friends have kept a distance from me, and community members have kept some secrets of what is also. I'm grateful to know we continue together on Earth asking we be global, and not just local citizens.

If to mention the top five online mentors and guides in this section, I think of Gary, Gabby, Lewis, Jack, and Christy. There are much more than a few I've not mentioned. Dan Holguin, Florencia, and Alexandra are three I think of, and I hope they continue to develop the correct channels for activating their dreams. If *I* want to reach thousands of sales of my books, I shall need to learn how to react to the amount of attention that a vast active audience gives.

And, for those that I don't yet know, though have read into these pages or my other books, thank you. I may not be as direct as I'd like to be, though amazing grace, peace, love, unity, and respect for you each too. Please keep your hearts open and glad, and I hope you also may find your dreams, wishes, and hopes become something awesomely rad!

Robert Koyich – December 2nd, 2018

148

Books, Contact Info, and Links

Fragments of Intent (The Fountains of Yesterday)
Compiled from the first three Fountains

The Sands of Yesterday (The Fountains of Faith)
A compilation of the 4th, 5th, and 6th Fountains

Shards of My Soul (The Fountains of Fortitude)
This three-part book combining the 7th, 8th, and 9th Fountains

Mosaic of Miracles (The Fountains of Fantasy)
This three-part book combining the 10th, 11th, and 12th Fountains

The Waters of Life (The Fountains of Flourishing)
This three-part book combining the 13th, 14th, and 15th Fountains

Shared Node (Key to Me)
A book of rhymes sourced from keystyles (pages of written verse)

Leading Up to A Year in Change
Rob's literal day to day journal for 2020

Introversial Mailing List
https://mailchi.mp/robertkoyich/introversial

For Donating to The Giving Group
To assist with providing routine grocery card support. please go to
https://donorbox.org/fountain-donations.
You may also send PayPal or e-transfers to ProvidingPoint@Gmail.com

For Supporting Rob through his Patreon page
www.Patreon.com/RobertKoyich

Please find and follow Robert Koyich on Goodreads

For email, message Robert@RobertKoyich.com (no PayPal)

Manufactured by Amazon.ca
Bolton, ON